VOICES OF THE HOLOCAUST

Perfection Learning®

EDITORIAL DIRECTOR   Julie A. Schumacher, Carol Francis

SENIOR EDITOR   Terry Ofner

EDITORS   Michael McGhee
Cecelia Munzenmaier

PERMISSIONS   Laura Pieper

REVIEWERS   Jacqueline Frerichs
Claudia A. Katz
Sue Ann Kuby
Ann L. Tharnish

DESIGN AND PHOTO RESEARCH   William Seabright and Associates,
Wilmette, Illinois

COVER ART   WARSAW 1952 Ben Shahn   The Hebrew text
incorporated into the painting is taken from the "Ten Martyrs' Prayer"
said on the Day of Atonement: "These I remember, and my soul melts
with sorrow, for strangers have devoured us like unturned cakes,
for in the days of the tyrant there was no reprieve for the [ten] martyrs
murdered by the government."   Shahn omitted the word 'ten'
(which referred to martyrs killed by the Romans) to make the quote
applicable to the Holocaust.

ACKNOWLEDGMENTS
"An Anti-Semitic Demonstration" by Gail Newman. Reprinted from
Ghosts of the Holocaust: An Anthology of Poetry by the Second Generation,
edited by Stewart J. Florsheim, by permission of the Wayne State University
Press. First appeared in Eva Poole-Gilson et al., eds., *Thread Winding in
the Loom of Eternity: California Poets in the Schools State-wide Anthology,
1987* (California Poets in the Schools, 1987).
"The Ball" from *Friedrich* by Hans Peter Richter, translated by Edite Kroll.
Copyright © Leonore Richter-Stiehl. Reprinted with permission of Leonore
Richter-Stiehl.   CONTINUED ON PAGE 159

95148
PB ISBN: 978-0-7891-8374-3
HB ISBN: 978-1-61383-202-8

Printed in the United States of America

Could a Holocaust Happen Here?

The question above is the *essential question* that you will consider as you read this book. The literature, activities, and organization of the book will lead you to think critically about this question and to develop a deeper understanding of the Holocaust.

To help you shape your answer to the broad essential question, you will read and respond to five sections, or clusters. Each cluster addresses a specific question and thinking skill.

CLUSTER ONE How could the Holocaust happen? **ANALYZE**

CLUSTER TWO How were victims oppressed? **COMPARE/CONTRAST**

CLUSTER THREE Was there resistance? **GENERALIZE**

CLUSTER FOUR Why should we remember? **SYNTHESIZE**

CLUSTER FIVE Thinking on your own

Notice that the final cluster asks you to think independently about your answer to the essential question—*Could a holocaust happen here?*

VOICES OF THE

First they came for the Jews

and I did not speak out

because I was not a Jew.

Then they came for the Communists

and I did not speak out

because I was not a Communist.

Then they came for the trade unionists

and I did not speak out

because I was not a trade unionist.

Then they came for me

and there was no one left

to speak out for me.

—Pastor Martin Niemöller

*(who spent seven years in concentration camps
after protesting the Nazi mistreatment of Jews)*

HOLOCAUST

TABLE OF CONTENTS

ANTI-SEMITISM:
A HISTORY OF HATE

nti-Semitism means prejudice against Jews. People who are anti-Semites don't want their children to marry or even be friends with Jews. Anti-Semites don't like to buy from Jewish businesses. Some anti-Semites burn crosses on the lawns of Jewish homes and paint swastikas on their temples. They blame Jews for everything that's wrong and believe Jews are too smart or too rich or own too much land.

If you were a Jew in ancient times, you might have been enslaved by the Egyptians. You couldn't be a citizen in the ancient Roman Empire. If you were a Jew, Christians sometimes called you "Christ killer," an allegation so inflammatory that it became the rallying cry of anti-Semitism for centuries.

If you were a Jew in the Middle Ages, you were often forced to live in a walled ghetto. Non-Jews didn't want you to influence them or their children and merchants didn't want your businesses competing with theirs. Outside the gates of your ghetto, you were required to wear an identifying badge.

At the outbreak of the plague called the Black Death (1348), you might have been accused of poisoning the water. If you were a Jew in 15th-century Spain, the Inquisition, a series of religious trials, could have expelled you or worse.

If you were a German Jew in 1879, you would have been a target of Wilhelm Marr who taught that Germans belonged to the Aryan "master race," while Jews were by nature a "slave race." Marr founded the League of Anti-Semitism to keep Germany from being "taken over" by Jews.

If you were a Russian Jew in 1881, *pogroms*, or organized attacks, might have caused you and hundreds of thousands of others to emigrate to the United States or to establish colonies in Palestine.

In 1923, an embittered, young soldier named Adolf Hitler was jailed for his part in a failed government coup. Hitler used his prison time to write *Mein Kampf* (My Struggle), a book filled with his plans for the creation of the Nazi party and world domination, his belief in Aryan superiority, and, most ominously, his fanatical anti-Semitism.

Upon release from prison, Hitler and a group of devoted followers began to preach the philosophy of Nazism. An explosive combination of economic depression in Germany and Hitler's powerful blend of treachery and inflammatory speechmaking led to his appointment as Chancellor in 1933. In 1934 he was elected president and named himself *Führer* or supreme leader.

Once in power Hitler turned anti-Semitism into an official government policy. Within a decade that policy had led to the murder of nearly 6 million European Jews as well as gypsies, intellectuals, homosexuals, handicapped Marxists, and other "enemies of the state." While millions were murdered outright through the use of gas chambers and other methods of extermination, hundreds of thousands of others died from disease, starvation, and slave labor.

FACES OF THE HOLOCAUST

Allied leaders meet at Yalta, in Russia. (From left) **Winston Churchill (1875-1965)** British Prime Minister; **Franklin Roosevelt (1882-1945)** U.S. President; **Josef Stalin (1879-1953)** Dictator of Soviet Russia

Oskar Schindler (1908-1974)
German businessman who first profited from the war but later became a hero by saving 1300 Jewish workers from the gas chambers.

Adolf Hitler (1889-1945)
Führer und Reichskanzler.
He promised glory for the Germans and destruction for the Jews.

Anne Frank (1929-1945)
Her diary, written while hiding from the Nazis, brought the horror of the Holocaust to the world.

Simon Wiesenthal (1908-)
A Holocaust survivor, he gave up a career in architecture to become a relentless Nazi hunter.

MAJOR EVENTS OF WORLD WAR II AND THE HOLOCAUST

1933

January
★Adolf Hitler appointed Chancellor of Germany

March
Dachau concentration camp opens

April
One-day boycott of Jewish shops and businesses; Gestapo (German internal security police) established

May
Public burnings of books written by Jews, political dissidents, and others not approved by the state

1935

May
Jews barred from serving in German army

September
★"Nuremberg Laws" passed. As a result, Jews no longer considered German citizens; Jews could not marry Aryans *perfect human* nor could they fly the German flag

1937

July
Buchenwald concentration camp opens

1934

August
★Hitler proclaims himself *Führer und Reichskanzler* (Leader and Reich Chancellor)

1936

March
Jewish doctors barred from practicing medicine in German institutions

August
Juden Verboten (No Jews) signs displayed outside many towns are removed during the Olympic Games in Berlin

★Jesse Owens African American Winner of Track Olymics

1938

March
★Hitler annexes Austria
9 million

August
Italy enacts sweeping anti-Semitic laws

October
Germans mark all Jewish passports with a large *J* to restrict Jews from leaving the country

September
Munich Agreement: Britain and France accept German takeover of part of Czechoslovakia

October
17,000 Polish Jews expelled from Germany

November
Kristallnacht (9–10) Decree forces all Jews to transfer retail businesses to Aryan hands. All Jewish pupils expelled from German schools

★ Sudetenland Czech Rubplic Invade Is

1932 President of US- FDR

"Broken Glass"

1941 *gas chambers*

June
Germany invades the Soviet Union

July
Hitler appoints Reinhard Heydrich to implement the "Final Solution of the Jewish Question"

September
34,000 Jews massacred at Babi Yar outside Kiev, Russia

December
Japanese attack Pearl Harbor, Hawaii; United States declares war on Japan and Germany

1939 *Holocaust begins*

September
Germany invades Poland; *line-up & shoot* World War II begins

November
Jews in German-occupied Poland forced to wear an arm band or yellow star

1943

April
Warsaw Ghetto revolt begins

August
Revolt at death camp in Treblinka, Poland

1945

April
Hitler commits suicide

May
V-E (Victory in Europe) Day: Germany surrenders; end of Third Reich

August
First atomic bomb dropped on Hiroshima, Japan

September
Japan surrenders; end of World War II

1940

April
Germany invades Denmark and Norway

May
Germany invades Holland, Belgium, and France; concentration camp established at Auschwitz

June
France surrenders

August
Battle of Britain (Germany's attempt to bomb Britain into submission) begins

1942

January
Heydrich outlines plan to murder Europe's Jews; German 6th Army surrenders at Stalingrad

October
Armed revolt in Sobibor extermination camp

1944

June
D-Day: Allied invasion at Normandy, France

July
Group of German officers attempts to assassinate Hitler; Russians liberate Maidanek killing center

October
Revolt by inmates at Auschwitz

CONCEPT VOCABULARY

You will find the following terms and definitions useful as you read and discuss the selections in this book.

Aryan race "Aryan" was originally applied to people who spoke any Indo-European language (in India, western Asia, and Europe). The Nazis, however, primarily used the term to refer to people of Northern European racial ancestry—especially those with blue eyes and blonde hair.

concentration camp Upon their ascent to power on January 30, 1933, the Nazis established concentration camps for the imprisonment of all "enemies" of their regime: political opponents, Jehovah's Witnesses, gypsies, homosexuals, and other "asocials." Beginning in 1938, Jews were targeted for internment solely because they were Jews.

Final solution The cover name for the plan to destroy the Jews of Europe— the "Final Solution of the Jewish Question." It began in December, 1941. Jews were rounded up and sent to extermination camps in the East. The program was deceptively disguised as "resettlement."

genocide The deliberate and systematic destruction of a religious, racial, national, or cultural group of people.

ghetto The Nazis revived the concept of medieval ghetto in creating their compulsory "Jewish Quarter." The ghetto was a section of a city where all Jews from the surrounding areas were forced to reside, surrounded by barbed wire or walls.

Nazi From the German words for Na(tional-so)zi(alist). A nazi was a member or supporter of the National Socialist Party in Germany led by Adolf Hitler.

propaganda ideas or claims spread deliberately to further one's cause or to damage an opponent's cause.

scapegoat a person or group that bears the blame for others. Scapegoating is the process of blaming others for one's problems.

Third Reich the German state during the Nazi period.

CLUSTER ONE

How Could the Holocaust Happen?
Thinking Skill   ANALYZING

Boy in front of a synagogue. Mukachevo (Ukraine), 1937.

The Ball

HANS PETER RICHTER

We ran along the street. Friedrich kept close to the houses; I stayed on the curb. I threw the little rubber ball I'd been given in the shoe store. It hit the center of the sidewalk and bounced high. Friedrich caught it and threw it back to me.

"My father will be home any moment!" he called to me. "I must get back soon. We're going shopping today. Maybe someone'll give me a ball, too!"

I nodded and jumped over a manhole. I waited until a pedestrian had gone by, then hurled the ball back to Friedrich.

Friedrich hadn't been watching.

There was a crash.

The ball rolled harmlessly back to me.

Friedrich stared openmouthed at the smashed shop window. I bent to pick up the ball, not yet believing what had happened.

Suddenly the woman stood before us. She grabbed Friedrich's arm and began to screech.

Doors and windows opened. A crowd gathered.

"Thieves! Burglars!" the woman shouted.

Her husband stood by the shop door, hands in his pockets, smoking a pipe.

"This good-for-nothing Jewboy here broke my shop window," she told everyone who cared to listen. "He wants to rob me." She turned to Friedrich. "But you didn't quite make it this time, did you. Because I'm always watching. I know you, you won't get away from me. You pack of Jews, they should get rid of you. First you ruin our business with your department stores, then you rob us on top of it! Just you wait, Hitler will show you yet!" And she shook Friedrich violently.

"But he didn't do it!" I yelled. "I threw the ball, I broke your window. We didn't want to steal!"

The woman looked at me, eyes large and stupid. Her mouth dropped open.

Her husband had swept the broken glass into the gutter. He collected the rolls of thread, the stars of black and white yarn, the balls of colorful embroidery yarn from the display case and carried them into the shop.

The woman's eyes grew very small. "How dare you interfere? What are you doing here anyway? Away with you! You don't think you have to protect this rotten Jewboy because you're living in the same house, do you? Go on, beat it!"

"But I threw the ball!" I said again.

The woman lunged at me, without letting go of Friedrich. Friedrich cried. He wiped his tears on his sleeve, smearing his whole face.

Someone had called the police.

Out of breath and sweating, a policeman arrived on a bicycle. He asked the woman to tell him what had happened.

Again she told the story of the attempted burglary.

I tugged at his sleeve. "Officer," I said, "he didn't do it. I broke the pane with my ball."

The woman looked at me threateningly. "Don't you believe him, Officer!" she said. "He only wants to protect the Jewboy here. Don't you believe him. He thinks the Jew's his friend just because they live in the same house."

The policeman bent down to me. "You don't understand this yet, you're too young still," he explained. "You may think you're doing him a favor by standing up for him. But you know he's a Jew. Believe me, we grownups have had plenty of experiences with Jews. You can't trust them; they're sneaky and they cheat. This woman was the only one who saw what happened, so . . . ."

"But she didn't see it!" I interrupted him. "Only I was there, and I did it!"

The policeman frowned. "You wouldn't try to call this woman a liar." I wanted to explain, but he didn't let me.

He took Friedrich's wrist from the woman and led him toward our house, followed by the woman and a long line of curious onlookers.

I joined the line.

Halfway there we ran into Herr Schneider.

Sobbing, Friedrich shouted, "Father!"

Astonished, Herr Schneider surveyed the procession. He came closer, said hello, and looked from one person to another, obviously puzzled.

"Your son—" said the policeman.

But the woman didn't give him a chance to go on. In one burst she repeated her tales. The only part she left out this time was her insinuation about Jews.

Herr Schneider listened patiently. When she had finished, he took Friedrich's chin in his hand and lifted his head so he could look into his eyes.

"Friedrich," he asked seriously, "did you break the shop window intentionally?"

Friedrich shook his head, still sobbing.

"I did it, Herr Schneider. I threw the ball, but I didn't do it on purpose!" And I showed him my small rubber ball.

Friedrich nodded.

Herr Schneider took a deep breath. "If you can swear on oath that what you just told me is the truth," he told the woman, "go ahead and register a formal complaint. You know me, and you know where I live!"

The woman did not reply.

Herr Schneider pulled out his purse. "Kindly release my son, Officer!" he said sharply. "I will pay for the damage at once." ❧

Recruiting poster for Hitler's National Student Organization. Translation at top left: "The German Student"; at bottom: "Fight for your leader and the people."

Serving *Mein Führer*

Eleanor Ayer

*The following biography tells about Alfons Heck's experience in
the Hitler Youth organization. The author, Eleanor Ayer, uses indented,
smaller print to indicate Heck's exact words.*

On the cool, windy afternoon of April 20, 1938, Adolf Hitler's forty-ninth
birthday, I was sworn into *Jungvolk,* the junior branch of the Hitler
Youth. When I raised three fingers of my right hand to the sky in the oath
to *der Führer*, my left hand gripping the flag of my unit, my spine tingled.

"I promise in the Hitler Youth to do my duty at all times in love and
faithfulness to help the *Führer*—so help me God."

The last line carried a message that turned out to be true for many of us:
"Our Banner Means More to us Than Death."

This bond of death, pledged by Alfons and millions of other young
Germans, was rooted in a deep love for the Fatherland. *Deutschland über
Alles* (Germany Over All) the national anthem proclaimed. Now, with the
dear Fatherland supposedly threatened by the evil Jews and gypsies,
millions of German teens rallied to its rescue. The Hitler Youth brought
them together as one strong force, ready to fight for their *Führer.*

Perhaps because he himself had dropped out at an early age, Adolf
Hitler did not consider school the most important part of a child's
education. Far more important was the *Jungvolk* (Young Folk), which chil-
ldren could join when they turned ten. Starting at age six, they could
become *Pimpfs,* apprentices in the *Jungvolk.* Careful records were kept of

their performance. Leaders wrote reports about the children's progress in athletics, camping, behavior, and—most important—their understanding of Nazi beliefs. If their records were good, they would be admitted to the *Jungvolk*. But before they could join, they must first pass a *Mutprobe*, or test of courage.

> The members of my *Schar*, a unit of about forty to fifty boys, were required to dive head first off the three-meter board—about ten feet high—into the town's swimming pool. There were some stinging belly flops, but the pain was worth it. When we passed the test, the fifteen-year-old leader of our company handed us the coveted dagger with the inscription "Blood and Honor" on its blade, meaning that we were fully accepted members of the *Jungvolk*.

Children didn't need their parents' permission to join the Hitler Youth. In fact, an adult who tried to keep a child from joining could be sent to prison. Nazi leaders didn't encourage parents to have their children join. Instead they spoke directly to the children, building in them a burning desire to be part of this great new movement. "You are a superior race of people," Hitler Youth leaders preached to their young recruits. "It is natural that you should rule the world." All this praise and promise of a glorious future inspired millions of children to join.

Parents who didn't agree with Hitler Youth leaders' ideas found themselves powerless to change their children's minds. Alfons's father was one who didn't agree. On a rare visit to the family farm, Jakob saw his son in uniform for the first time.

> Wildly he shook his fist at me. "You have all the makings of an arrogant Nazi," he shouted. "They're going to bury you in that monkey suit, *Du verdammter Idiot.*" But I looked coldly through him and walked away. I was beyond his crazy ranting and raving.

Girls as well as boys were attracted by the power, glory, and importance that the Hitler Youth promised. While boys served in the *Jungvolk*, girls became *Jungmädel* (Young Maidens). Their uniforms were white blouses with ties and full blue skirts, often highlighted by the not-too-ladylike heavy marching shoes. Boys' uniforms looked much like those of the SA, the Storm Troopers. Around the upper left arm of their brown shirts they wore an armband bearing the black Nazi swastika inside a white diamond, on a field of red and white. Pants were black, bermuda short length, and were worn with white knee socks.

Girls' training was much the same as boys' and included long hours of marching and hiking. But there was one important difference. From the beginning, girls were taught that their most important duty to the Fatherland was to become mothers of healthy Aryan German babies. It was best if they could marry and then become mothers. But often motherhood was stressed so strongly that girls became pregnant before marriage—as part of their "duty" to the Fatherland.

Within the Hitler Youth, there were several divisions, just as there were in the *Wehrmacht* or regular army. Alfons belonged to the *Fanfarenzug,* the drum and fanfare platoon.

> During parades, the *Fanfarenzug* always preceded any large units of the Hitler Youth in order to set the marching rhythm. Hundreds of boys were arranged in formation ahead of the flawlessly goose-stepping soldiers who followed. The *Wehrmacht* tried to keep cordial relations with the Hitler Youth because we were its pool of future manpower. There was never a single rally without us. We were the icing on the cake.

Such fanfare at public gatherings delighted the German people, and Hitler's men were masters at it. When the Nazis staged an event, it was always a spectacular show. For Alfons Heck, the summer of 1938 ended in the grandest show of all, "before which everything else in my short life paled. . . . It would bind me to Adolf Hitler until the bitter end."

Although he had been a member of the *Jungvolk* for only five months, Alfons was chosen to attend the Nuremberg Party Congress or *Reichsparteitag,* the "high mass" of Nazism. For centuries Nuremberg, in the southern state of Bavaria, had been the showcase city of German history. The Nazis used it as the annual gathering spot for hundreds of thousands of loyal followers. A huge tent city was set up, and for seven days people attended rallies praising Adolf Hitler, the power of the Nazis, and the glory of the new Germany. "Even for a ten-year-old," recalled Alfons, "it was a near feverish, week-long high that lasted into one's dreams."

> The Day of the Hitler Youth was Saturday, September 10: Shortly before noon, 80,000 Hitler Youth were lined up in rows as long as the entire stadium. The tension among us tingled into our fingertips. When Hitler finally appeared, we greeted him with a thundering, triple *"Sieg Heil,"* (Hail to Victory) and it took all of our discipline to end it there, as we had been instructed.

Hitler, the superb actor that he was, always began his speeches quietly, almost man to man. Then his voice rose, took on power, and his right fist punctuated the air in a series of short, powerful jabs. "You, my youth," he shouted, with his eyes seeming to stare right at me, "are our nation's most precious guarantee for a great future. You are destined to be the leaders of a glorious new order under National Socialism! You, my youth," he screamed hoarsely, "never forget that one day you will rule the world."

For minutes on end, we shouted at the top of our lungs, with tears streaming down our faces: *"Sieg Heil, Sieg Heil, Sieg Heil!"* From that moment on, I belonged to Adolf Hitler body and soul.

Three days later, during Nazi Party Day ceremonies at Nuremberg, speaking on the theme of Greater Germany, Hitler issued a warning. He was talking about the neighboring country of Czechoslovakia and the Germans who lived in its northern region, the Sudetenland. He spoke of "the oppression," the unfair treatment, that Sudeten Germans were suffering at the hands of the Czech government. "If these tortured creatures cannot gain rights and assistance by themselves," he warned, "they can get both from us."

All this talk of oppression was just an excuse. What Hitler really wanted was to invade Czechoslovakia so he could gain more land, *Lebensraum,* for his people. And the *Führer* was used to getting what he wanted.

Just six months earlier, at dawn on March 12, German army troops had crossed into Austria, the border country of Adolf Hitler's birth. His purpose at that time, he claimed, was "to restore my dear homeland to the German Reich." Most Austrians welcomed the *Führer*. They were delighted with what they called *Anschluss* or "reunification of the Germanic people." Austrians and Germans were now one again, as they had been earlier in history. It was a quiet takeover. Without losing one life, Adolf Hitler added nine million people and vast new lands to the Third Reich.

Now, as he prepared to enter Czechoslovakia, people remembered the Austrian *Anschluss*. Many began to ask themselves just how far the *Führer* planned to go. But Hitler was quick to promise that this would be his last move into other countries. Once he gained back the Sudetenland, he assured them, he would seek no new territory. Common people and world leaders alike believed him. That is why no one made a move to help the Czechs on October 1, 1938, when German troops invaded the Sudetenland.

German crowds salute a parade of Hitler youth.

The Czech people did not welcome Hitler as the Austrians had done. But although Czechoslovakia had an army nearly as strong as the *Wehrmacht*, it could not hold out against the Germans. Within days, Adolf Hitler had accomplished another easy victory, and brought an additional three and one-half million people under his control. With the Sudetenland under his belt, Hitler laughed off his promise of no more invasions. Within six months, he had taken over all of Czechoslovakia.

Hitler Youth members went wild with pride and excitement. These easy victories were certain proof of the strength and superiority of the Fatherland. It was obvious to most teenagers that Hitler was invincible—he could not be beaten. In their minds, *der Führer* was more powerful than God. Alfons Heck was one of those firm followers.

Death was merely an abstract idea to us youngsters. Germany was a country of sun-flecked, unlimited promise. If Hitler had died that year, he would have been celebrated as one of the greatest statesmen of German history, despite his hatred of the Jews. No world leader of the time approached Hitler's ability to draw the praise of his people. I watched women become hysterical and faint when he smiled at them.

Hitler's hatred of Jews didn't dampen his image in most people's minds. Good Aryans paid little attention to their hero's darker side. Few of them objected to the many unfair laws that were now being forced upon the Jews. One of the newest demanded that all German Jews use only Jewish first names. If you were Jewish with a common first name like Karl or Heidi, the Nazis said you must change it to something "obviously Jewish" like Abraham or Sarah so you could be identified more easily.

All across Germany, the fate of the Jews was beginning to look more and more bleak. Headlines like this one screamed off the pages of the *Völkischer Beobachter,* the Nazi Party newspaper:

JEWS, ABANDON ALL HOPE!
OUR NET IS SO FINE THAT THERE IS NOT A HOLE
THROUGH WHICH YOU CAN SLIP.

Alfons's former school friend, Heinz Ermann, was among those whose families heeded the dire warnings. Like thousands of other Jewish families, the Ermanns frantically took steps to slip through the net.

One afternoon, Heinz came to our farm, all dressed up in his best velvet suit, to say good-bye. "My Uncle Herbert is taking me with him for a while," he said sadly. Uncle Herbert was a rabbi in the city of Cologne.

"Maybe that's best, Heinz," said my grandmother. "It'll be nice for you seeing a big city." Heinz's father had decided to send his only son away, since it was impossible for a Jewish child to go unnoticed in a small town. Sooner or later, somebody in Wittlich would call Heinz a dirty Jew—or worse—and his father wanted to spare him that.

My grandmother gave us a piece of cake, normally a Sunday treat, and then we shook hands awkwardly. *"Auf Wiedersehen, Frau Heck,"* Heinz said, but he just nodded to me. We both knew that our friendship had ended. Later, when I had to go through interviews for promotions in the Hitler Youth, I always denied having had a Jew for a friend. Before long, Heinz had become just a fleeting memory. ∾

Afterword

In an Emmy-winning film, Alfons Heck reflects on his former loyalty to Adolf Hitler. Confessions of a Hitler Youth *was filmed in 1992.*

I'm proud that I have found the courage to speak out about my own past. By telling people what really happened, by helping them understand the Nazi era from the point of view of the perpetrator, I hope I can help to prevent such a disaster from ever happening again.

I try to explain *how* it was possible for people as educated and cultured as the Germans to follow a man like Hitler. How could this happen in Germany? Because we simply did not care enough for other people. We didn't care about anything else except ourselves.

When I speak to young people, the message I hope that they must remember is this: the murder of eleven million people in the Holocaust began very simply with prejudice, minor harassment. If you allow harassment to grow and fester, if you do nothing to stop it, then *you* become one of the perpetrators. What began in the Hitler years as minor harassment turned, in the end, to genocide.

Family Album

Amos Neufeld

My father stands in the picture
with his parents, brothers and sisters.
(The gas and sealed cattle-cars
are still two years away.) They smile
not knowing this is the last time
they will be gathered happily together,
that nothing guards their world,
that sky will be all that remains.

Their eyes rest peacefully
on one another and on the camera
while tomorrow winds its arms
and twists tighter round their necks.
Yet it is still too early
to see the black boots coming:
smoke floats carelessly from a cigarette
and children go to summer camp.

We see them—not yet lost,
standing on the precipice of wind and fire,
their image of vanished innocence,
captured and in our memory engraved.
Still they stand, unsuspecting,
composed, like any other happy family,
while their black and white world rushes toward. . . .
is already on the final page.

Family Hanukkah celebration. Leipzig, Germany, 1934.

An Anti-Semitic Demonstration

GAIL NEWMAN

from a photograph by Roman Vishniac

There are hundreds of people in the street.
This could be New York or Chicago.
Traffic is stopped in the cold.
The men are bare-headed, wearing long
heavy coats, and some of them are running
with raised arms, their flat palms lifted
like white slashes against the sky. The dark
bodies move in formation across that ordinary
street, a street with lamp posts and gutters,
a street with automobiles and drug stores and stains
that could be the scuff marks of hundreds of shoes
marching, or car oil, or blood.
The faces of the crowd are far away and small
with features indistinct as smudged charcoal.
I don't know the name of this street,
but I know it is Poland, 1938, and my mother
may be living close by, listening at the window
with the shades drawn, listening to the future
rushing toward her like a wave, listening to her heart
beat against her sixteen year old breast like a finger
tapping on glass.
I'd like to push this crowd back along the narrow
littered street, back into the past
when my mother's arm was still bare, before
a blue number was branded there.

An anti-Semitic demonstration
in Warsaw, Poland, 1938.
Photo by Roman Vishniac.

Broken Glass, Broken Lives

Arnold Geier

I t was the spring of 1915. The battle was ferocious. One German soldier, preparing to sprint ahead, suddenly caught a bullet, screamed, and fell. About twenty yards behind him, another soldier slowly dragged him by the belt toward a trench at the rear. Medics were waiting with a canvas stretcher and carried the bleeding soldier away.

In wartime, this was not an unusual incident, and it was soon forgotten.

For Jews in Germany, 1938 was not a good year. Special laws, specifically aimed against them, had been passed in the last two years, limiting the social, political, and economic activities of their daily lives. The handwriting was on the wall, but not all Jews saw it clearly. Although some had left as soon as Hitler had come to power, others were convinced that the political winds would change and that persecution belonged to bygone days and would never be revived by a civilized nation in the 20th Century. Many had made contacts with relatives, friends, and organizations hoping to find someone to sponsor them for emigration to a specific country or to any country that would have them. So it was not unusual to hear of a Jew in Germany who was planning to emigrate to the U.S., Shanghai, Colombia, Cuba, England, Palestine, or South Africa. But most Jews had no friends or relatives abroad and simply faced their uncertain future with trepidation mixed with hope.

My family was lucky. Mama's sister and her husband had moved to New York in the 1920s, in search for the "good life." My uncle worked as a night janitor in a skyscraper. The family lived in a low-rent state-supported apartment in Brooklyn. They had no money, but they had compassion, love, and courage. My aunt set out to help us by finding someone wealthy enough to qualify as a sponsor, as required by law. She called and searched all over New York. She pleaded, cajoled, and begged every prospect until she found one, an orthodox Jewish brassiere manufacturer, who was willing to sponsor our family and my grandparents and aunt for immigration to the U.S. This was no small task. It meant preparation of an "affidavit" consisting of disclosure of financial holdings, copies of tax returns, and a sworn guarantee that the sponsor would support the newcomers so they would not become a financial burden to the U.S. government.

In the fall of 1938, we received our affidavit on a Thursday, and Papa immediately brought it to the U.S. Embassy in Berlin to register it and to receive a number. My grandfather decided to hold his over the weekend and to have an attorney-friend verify that all was in order. When he brought it to the Embassy on Monday morning, the quota had closed. His affidavit was not accepted.

In a "Jewish area" of Berlin, Grandpa, Grandma, and Aunt Dora were in their apartment on the evening of November 8th, when they heard a firm knock on their door. Grandpa froze. In Germany, such knocks usually meant trouble. The knock sounded again. With fear and apprehension in his heart, Grandpa opened the door slightly. There stood a tall man with strong Germanic features, dressed in a gray suit. He seemed to crowd the door, casting furtive glances to each side, as if he did not want to be seen there. "May I come in, please." It was not a question but a command. Grandpa stepped back and the man quickly entered, closing the door behind him. He remained standing as if frozen to the spot. "*Herr*[1] Geier, I can only stay a minute." Grandpa held his breath. The man looked down, avoiding Grandpa's eyes. "Herr Geier, do you remember when you saved a soldier on the battlefield many years ago? I am that soldier." Like flood waters bursting a dam, almost forgotten memories overwhelmed Grandpa. At first, he had put the incident on the back-shelf of his mind. After the Nazis came to power, he had forced himself to forget it altogether. "I work with the Chief of Police in Berlin and have kept track of you for a long time. Listen carefully now. Tomorrow night, police and SS will round up adult male Jews all over Germany. I have seen the list, and your name is on it. Do whatever you wish." He paused. Now his eyes met Grandpa's. "My debt to you is paid. *Auf Wiedersehen!*"[2] And

---

1 **Herr**: German word for *Mister*.
2 **Auf Wiedersehen!**: Good-bye!

with that he turned, went through the door and disappeared into the darkness.

Grandpa was stunned. It took him several minutes to realize what had just happened. He trembled with fear and bewilderment, then quickly called my father and told him to come right over. He did not dare to say anything on the phone, so Papa was very concerned and took a taxi. Grandpa told him what happened, and both men knew they had to do something and quickly. After deliberating, they arrived at a plan. For the rest of that night and most of the following day, Grandpa and Papa were on their telephones spreading the news of the arrival in town that evening of Mr. Malach Hamoves (Hebrew for the angel of death). They suggested that he be greeted by all of our friends and their friends, and that news of his arrival be passed along to other interested parties. Those who were called presumably were warning their relatives and friends. Hundreds were probably contacted during those 12 hours. In late afternoon, Papa told us that he was going on a business trip for a while, kissed Mama, and left. To a 15-year-old girl and her 12-year-old brother, this didn't appear unusual. Actually, he took public transportation to the home of one of his customers, a self-professed anti-Nazi, who had offered to shelter him for a few days. So Papa spent the night there—to him it was the night of November 9th, 1938, and to history it would become Kristallnacht.[3]

Early the next morning, I was suddenly shaken out of my sleep by a large hand on my shoulder. The shock forced my sleepy eyes open. There above me was a man. He looked like a giant, in a black uniform with silver emblems and decorations. He shouted: "Where is your father!" I was never so scared in my life. The words barely left my lips. "He's on a business trip somewhere." The giant let go of my shoulder. He looked under my bed, in the closet, grumbled, and left to search the other areas of the apartment. When he found nothing, he confronted Mama with anger. I could hear her promise him, in a soft and pleasant voice, that she would have Papa call him as soon as he returned. Finally, the Nazi left. Mama quickly tried to calm us and assured us that everything would be all right. She rushed us to get dressed and have some breakfast.

While we were eating, the noise level from the street below seemed to swell. Suddenly, there were sounds of breaking glass, and a mixture

3 **Kristallnacht:** Literally, Night of the Broken Glass. Hitler ordered the SS to attack Jewish synagogues and businesses to see how the world would react. He then continued his efforts to eliminate all Jewish people in Germany.

Man seeking emigration assistance from the Mutual Aid Society for German Jews. Berlin, Germany, 1938.

of shouts, orders, and laughter, blending with screams of terror. We rushed to the window, three stories above the street, and saw hundreds of men, women, and children milling about, watching groups of storm-troopers in action. One was smashing the windows of nearby shops, destroying their displays, and painting their walls with Stars of David and anti-Semitic slogans. DIE JEW! DON'T BUY FROM JEWS! THE JEWS ARE OUR MISFORTUNE! Another group was beating a bearded elderly Jew with nightsticks and bare fists. When I saw the blood streaming from the old man's face as his beard was being pulled off, I went wild. "No, no, leave him alone!" I screamed out the window in my 12-year-old voice. Of course, my plea was promptly lost in the tumult below. The police stood nearby and watched. No one interfered. Mama pulled me away from the window, held me and my sister close to her bosom, and I cried like I had never cried before. Where was Papa? I wondered.

My father had spent the night with his German customer, hoping that Grandpa's alarm was a false one. By early morning, the radio news reports of a "spontaneous citizens' outburst" against Jews all over the city and throughout the country convinced Papa it was all true.

He had formulated a plan. He was afraid to remain with his German host. It was dangerous for both. He wasn't sure just how anti-Nazi this family would be if circumstances put them to the test. Papa had heard that the authorities did not bother Jews who had a visa[4] to another country. As far as Germany was concerned, they were considered gone—good riddance. The American Embassy had our affidavits, and Papa had an official number with the embassy. That's where, he figured, he must go.

The American Embassy did not open until 9 a.m., so Papa had to use up at least two hours. He rode whatever trolleys and busses were operating, and changed from time to time so as to appear like a normal commuter and not to arouse suspicion. When it came closer to 9 o'clock, he took the bus which went into the central area and past the American Embassy. As the bus approached, he was surprised to see hundreds of people, many still in their pajamas and robes, jammed against the front and garden gates, trying to push them open. On the other side, on American soil, several people stood around watching the events, but they did not open the gates. On the fringes of the mob, Gestapo and SS men were picking up screaming and struggling figures and were dragging them to waiting trucks. It was 20 minutes before 9.

Papa continued on the bus for exactly ten more minutes. Then he got off, crossed the street, and boarded another bus going back toward the embassy. If his calculation was correct, he would arrive there at precisely 9 a.m. He did. As he stepped off the bus, the embassy gates were opened and a flood of people poured onto the grounds. There was no stopping them. The Gestapo and SS men were shoved aside and Papa joined in the mob and pushed his way through with the others. For the moment, he was on American soil, safe from German authority.

The embassy people were sympathetic and did what they could. They brought in food, allowed the pathetic crowd to stand and sit in the door-

4 **visa:** document that allows a traveler to enter a foreign country.

ways, halls, and gardens, and tried to calm frightened adults and children. After several hours, Papa finally managed to get the attention of one of the embassy clerks. He told her that he had an official visa number and pleaded with her to arrange an appointment with an officer. The young woman reminded him that there was little work being accomplished under the circumstances, but she promised to do what she could. He never saw her again. He gave up hope. At 5 p.m., the embassy was ready to close. Hundreds of people still lingered on the grounds. They refused to leave. A high-ranking American embassy official rushed out of his protective office to plead with the crowd. Papa intercepted him in the hall, grabbed his sleeve, and held on. With tears in his eyes, he told him of his visa number and begged the official to have our number changed into an actual visa there and then. The bewildered man looked at Papa, at the crowd he was about to face, back at Papa, and motioned to an assistant. "See this man now," he directed, "and if he checks out, give him his visa."

Within an hour, Papa was the proud owner of a precious American visa. It was no more that a large rubber stamp on one page of his passport, with names and dates of birth inserted, but, in Germany on this day, it was life itself. Papa came home. On the way, he was stopped several times, showed his visa, and was left alone.

I never learned the fate of the others who had fled to the security of the American Embassy that day. Grandpa had hidden with a German family on the outskirts of the city and returned only after the pogrom[5] had calmed down. He had an unused affidavit. He never obtained an official number for a visa, because the quota was never reopened. Grandpa, Grandma, and Aunt Dora did not survive. Thanks to Papa's determination and courage, we did. ❧

---

5 **pogrom:** organized massacre of helpless peoples.

Crystal Night

LYN LIFSHIN

windows slashed
like skin pulled
tight   frozen with a
stone   slammed thru
it   smashed blue

glass   crystal   a
whole lake of ice
a plane crashes
into   smashed
tea cups   bowl of

glass   glass
shattering in the
night   something like
a mirror walked
into they came   beat

people up   blue
jars   the glass piled
in an alley calf
deep. All night the
sound of ice in

the branches poking
holes in the roof
A warning   stained
glass from the
synagogue slashed

plum   peach   cherry
frosting over in
the chill NOvember
light   an arm
torn   bleeding

a whole family
in shards and this
just the beginning

Cleaning up after
Kristallnacht
(Crystal Night), 1938.

Holocaust Memorial, Berlin, Germany, Europe

Fritz Gerlich's Spectacles

John Roth

As the 21st century unfolds, the Holocaust recedes farther into the past. As something that happened in an earlier century, it may appear to be increasingly distant from us. Nothing, however, could be further from the truth. The genocide happened: it casts shadows upon the earth. The genocide makes no darkness unthinkable, no destruction unimaginable, no devastation impossible. Post-Holocaust ethnic cleansing in Kosovo[1] and genocides in Bosnia[2] and Rwanda[3] testify to that. Only if the Holocaust's warning is heeded and not forgotten can the cry "never again!" keep from being mocked by a resounding "again and again!" The warning can be best heeded by starting at the beginning. We start by paying attention to broken eyeglasses that belonged to a German journalist named Fritz Gerlich.

1   **Kosovo:** A former territory of Serbia with a majority population of Albanians. In the late 1990s, Serbian forces displaced about one million Albanians and killed thousands of others when Albanians began to fight for independence. Albanians also forced about 100,000 Serbs and others from their homes. Leaders on both sides were brought to trial for heinous war crimes. Kosovo is now an independent state.

2   **Bosnia:** The country of Bosnia and Herzegovina, once part of Yugoslavia. It includes large populations of Bosnian Muslims (Bosniaks), Serbian Orthodox Christians, and Croatian Roman Catholics. In 1992 Bosniaks declared independence, a move opposed by most Serbs. The three-year war that followed resulted in more than 100,000 deaths. Among these were 8,000 Bosniak men and boys massacred at Srebrenica by Serbs. Leaders of the massacre have been tried by an international tribunal and several have been found guilty of genocide.

3   **Rwanda:** An East African country in which about 800,000 civilians, almost all belonging to the minority Tutsi ethnic group, were massacred by the governing Hutu in 1994.

Born in 1883, Dr. Fritz Gerlich grew up in Munich. There he studied university science and history, writing a dissertation on a medieval Germanic emperor to obtain his doctorate. Hampered by the poor eyes that led to his wearing the steel-rimmed spectacles for which he became well known, Gerlich was unable to serve in the German Army during World War I. Instead he worked in the national archives while becoming increasingly attracted to political journalism.

Staunchly defending German nationalism in the aftermath of his country's defeat in 1918, Gerlich soon became editor-in-chief of the *Münchener Neueste Nachrichten,*[4] one of the city's most conservative newspapers. By the early 1920s, Gerlich was a significant figure in Germany's postwar nationalist movement. In the spring of 1923, he received a visit from a controversial man, six years his junior, who was the leader of the right-wing National Socialist German Workers' Party. That man was Adolf Hitler.

Hitler's 1923 visit to Gerlich took place in troubled times. Saddled with the huge debt incurred in financing World War I and the misery of soaring inflation, the Weimar Republic (as the parliamentary government of Germany was called from 1919 to 1933) was stressed and strained. To glimpse what was to happen between Gerlich and Hitler, it is important to note in more detail a few of the reasons for Germany's distress at that time.

Germany's defeat in World War I was officially sealed on Armistice Day, November 11, 1918. Seven months later, on June 28, 1919, the Versailles Treaty, which established the peace terms, was signed in Paris. The treaty pronounced Germany guilty for starting the war and required the Germans to pay for all the damages the Allies had suffered. A reparations[5] commission would determine the amount. The terms of an agreement subsequently reached in London in May 1921 put Germany's war reparations bill at 132 billion gold marks (about $31 billion at the prevailing exchange rate). The debt was to be paid at six percent interest over 37 years. The annual payments would amount to two billion gold marks plus 26 percent of German exports. Estimated to be about seven percent of Germany's national income, the annual payments were judged by British economist John Maynard Keynes to be three times what the country could afford. The financial burden created deep

---

4 *Münchener Neueste Nachrichten:* newspaper titled *Munich Latest News.*

5 **reparations:** transfers of money and property to make amends for wrongdoing.

resentment that Hitler and his Nazi Party would exploit to the fullest.

From the beginning, Germany had difficulty meeting the reparations schedule. Already at the end of 1921, for example, the government declared that it could not make the payments due in January and February 1922. Several times Germany asked for a moratorium,[6] but France, in particular, saw payment defaults as an opportunity to weaken Germany further by reoccupying the Rhine-Ruhr area, a region of industrial and strategic importance for Germany's postwar recovery. On January 11, 1923, using a shortfall in German wood and coal delivery as his pretext, French Premier Raymond Poincare sent troops into that part of Germany to oversee French interests.

Unable to offer military resistance to the French occupation, which was augmented by Belgian forces, the Germans responded with passive resistance.[7] When 130,000 German laborers refused to work, the region's productivity declined by half. The French met this resistance with arrests, imprisonments, evictions, and even executions. By the summer of 1923, the woes of the slumping German economy had grown worse

Germans in the Ruhr region were encouraged to use passive resistance against French forces through posters such as this one, which reads, "No! You won't subdue me!"

and the French occupation force in the Rhine-Ruhr area had risen to 100,000 men, a number equivalent to the size permitted for the entire German Army by the Versailles Treaty. These outcomes added insult to German injury, especially for those who erroneously believed, as Hitler did, that Germany's defeat and especially the Versailles Treaty had been the result of a *Dolchstoss* ("stab in the back") inflicted from within Germany by Jewish traitors and their left-wing collaborators.

6 **moratorium:** legally authorized delay or waiting period.

7 **passive resistance:** nonviolent opposition to laws or practices.

Because the German mark lost so much value during the hard economic times, even bread became more expensive than many Germans could afford. Bread lines such as this one provided free food for hungry people.

In 1923 Germany experienced one of the most desperate inflationary spirals[8] any industrialized nation has known. The country's wartime financing had depended less on increased taxation and much more on loans and bonds, which then were repaid by the government's already inflationary policy of increasing the money in circulation at the time. As quickly as the paper money was printed, its value depreciated.

Unfortunately, the problems plaguing Germany's economy went well beyond both the debts that had accumulated during wartime and the reparations demands that were another immense price for defeat. The war had harmed Germany's industrial capacity. Its stock of raw materials and goods had been severely depleted. Then there were the high costs of converting the economy from wartime to peacetime operation, a difficulty compounded by Germany's high unemployment. That problem, in turn, was made no easier by the fact that in 1920 Germany still maintained 660,000 soldiers. To meet the provisions of the Versailles Treaty, 560,000 had to be demobilized[9] and then, somehow, absorbed into the German labor force. That goal could scarcely be accomplished in an economy whose inflationary instability was rapidly destroying confidence in the government. In the early 1920s, one dollar was worth 100 marks. In January 1923 the mark fell to 18,000 per dollar. Hyperinflation[10] had replaced inflation. Later in the year, the exchange rate soared to 4.2 billion marks to the dollar. Before the spiral could be brought under control at the end of 1923, the hyperinflation had ruined millions of ordinary Germans who depended on wages, fixed incomes, or savings that had been carefully accumulated during better times. At the inflation's peak, a liter of milk or a loaf of bread could cost billions of marks. Prices changed not only daily but *during* the day as well. Currency held in the morning was worthless by nightfall.

Hyperinflation benefited some financial manipulators who obtained huge bank loans, used them to buy businesses or property, and then were able to repay their loans with devalued currency. Most Germans, however, found themselves in dire economic straits, for it was not unusual for them to receive word from their banks indicating that their deposits no longer had any value.

8 **inflationary spirals:** economic patterns in which a variety of forces perpetuate a rise in general prices.

9 **demobilized:** taken out of military service.

10 **hyperinflation:** out-of-control inflation.

An early mecca for Germany's postwar nationalist movements, the region of Bavaria—and in particular Munich, its chief city—not only was affected by economic instability in 1923 but was also a place where plans to restore order by revolutionary means were under way. It is likely that such plans led to Hitler's meeting with the bespectacled Fritz Gerlich. Gerlich was no Nazi, but the two men shared interests, and they might have become allies. As it turned out, the opposite happened. Gerlich became one of Germany's most persistent and adamant[11] opponents of Hitler and the Nazis. The origin of his loathing for Hitler is less than crystal clear, but it probably stemmed from assurances that Hitler gave Gerlich in the spring and then broke in the autumn of 1923.

German Beer Hall Putsch

As Ron Rosenbaum documents the story in his 1998 book, *Explaining Hitler,* Gerlich backed the political aspirations of Gustav von Kahr, the right-wing nationalist governor of Bavaria. Hitler may have promised Gerlich that he, too, would support Kahr and not resort to illegal methods to advance the Nazi agenda. Subsequently, Gerlich witnessed the Munich Beer Hall *Putsch*[12] on November 8–9, 1923, in which Hitler rashly

11 **adamant:** unyielding.

12 ***Putsch:*** a secretly planned and sudden attempt to overthrow a government.

attempted a takeover of the Bavarian state. The coup[13] began on the evening of November 8, when Hitler and other Nazi Party leaders interrupted a patriotic meeting in Munich's *Bürgerbräukeller,*[14] where Kahr was the featured speaker. With Nazi Storm Troopers surrounding the building, Hitler put Kahr under arrest and extorted[15] his support at gunpoint.

Once Kahr was free of intimidation, he renounced his coerced support. He also directed Bavarian police forces to be ready by midday on November 9. That afternoon Hitler and other Nazi leaders—including General Erich Ludendorff, a German war hero, and Hermann Göring, an ace fighter pilot who would become a key figure in the Third Reich—advanced toward the *Odeonsplatz*[16] in Munich's center with some 2000 of their followers. Blocking the Nazis' path, the state police opened fire. Sixteen Nazis and four members of the police were killed. Hitler and Göring were injured. The coup failed, but far from forgetting it, the Nazis made this early revolutionary upsurge a key part of their party's identity. The fallen Nazis became martyrs. Those who survived became specially honored heroes among the *Alte Kümpfer* (old fighters), the Nazis who belonged to the Party before Hitler's rise to governmental power on January 30, 1933.

Meanwhile, Hitler was arrested two days after the failed coup. He stood trial for treason three months later. The court, however, was not overly concerned about Hitler's attempt to overthrow the government. Sentenced to five years in Landsberg Prison, Hitler was released after nine months, in December 1924. He had put his comfortable prison term to good use by starting to write one of the 20th century's most influential books, *Mein Kampf (My Struggle)*, which was published in 1925. By 1933 *Mein Kampf* had sold more than one million copies. The 500th printing took place in 1939, and by 1945 sales had reached ten million copies. The royalties[17] made Hitler a wealthy man.

13 **coup:** overthrow of power.

14 ***Bürgerbräukeller:*** a large beer hall.

15 **extorted:** took by force or coercion.

16 ***Odeonsplatz:*** a pedestrian square surrounded by buildings of cultural and historical importance.

17 **royalties:** payments based on a percentage of a book's earnings.

By 1933 Fritz Gerlich was a marked man as far as Hitler and the Nazis were concerned. For a decade, he had neither forgotten nor forgiven Hitler's broken promises. Gerlich never lost the conviction that had been driven home to him in 1923: namely, that deception, treachery, and ruthless violence were at the heart of Hitler's character. Gerlich determined that he would use his expertise and influence as a journalist to do his best to expose Hitler in any way he could.

Gerlich was not the only German journalist who opposed Hitler and the Nazi Party during the 1920s and early 1930s. Even before Gerlich used his pen against Hitler, a group of now largely (but undeservedly) forgotten editors and reporters at the *Munich Post*—Martin Gruber, Erhard Auer, Edmund Goldschagg, and Julius Zerfass among them—used a savvy combination of investigative and tabloid styles to expose the Nazis as scandal-ridden, blackmailing, murderous thugs who would stop at nothing to put their racist, antisemitic politics into practice. Arguably the first public voices raised against Hitler, their opposition was from the political left more than from Gerlich's conservative perspective, but their themes and his had much in common.

For 12 years, up to and even including Hitler's early days as Germany's chancellor in the winter of 1933, the *Munich Post* battled Hitler and the National Socialists in print. Regarding Hitler as a political criminal and the Nazis as a reckless gang, the newspaper portrayed Hitler as controlling every move the Nazis made. The Nazis, the *Post*'s journalists typically underscored, were the "Hitler Party." Its cartoons lampooned Hitler; its stories aimed to topple him. The paper exposed murderous blackmail-driven purges within the Nazi Party, and denounced Hitler's lie that a Socialist "stab in the back" had brought about Germany's World War I defeat. *Post* reporters implicated Hitler criminally in the mysterious death of his half-niece, Geli Raubal, and they insinuated that Hitler's antisemitism was unsuccessfully covering the likelihood that he was himself at least partly Jewish. In "The Jews in the Third Reich," a forecast published on December 9, 1931, more than two years before Hitler took power, the *Post* reported that it knew of a secret Nazi plan to deprive Jews of civil rights, confiscate their property, and achieve "the Final Solution of the Jewish Question" by removing them from German society through slave labor.

To carry out their "Final Solution," Nazis killed more than one million Jews at Auschwitz alone, the largest network of concentration and death camps.

In Nazi circles, the *Munich Post* became known as the "Poison Kitchen." Prior to the Nazi takeover in 1933, "the Hitler Party" tried to silence the *Post* with libel suits[18] and death threats against its staff. Nevertheless, the newspaper's anti-Nazi resistance continued. Well into February 1933, the *Post* continued to publish reports about political murders carried out by the Nazis. Among its final anti-Hitler accounts was a three-part series that valiantly tried to counter what the *Post* had long regarded as Hitler's most destructive characteristic: his willful falsification of history. The *Post* foresaw Hitler's aims as disastrous for Germany and the world. Its views, however, did not prevail. Before the 1932–33 winter had ended, the *Post*'s anti-Hitler reporting was smashed, its courageous journalists imprisoned or killed.

While the *Munich Post* attacked Hitler from the left, Fritz Gerlich and some of his journalistic colleagues became the most vociferous[19] anti-

18 **libel suits:** lawsuits charging that untruthful printed words caused harm to reputation.

19 **vociferous:** loud and insistent.

Hitler critics among German conservatives. Moving on from his position with the *Münchener Neueste Nachrichten,* Gerlich led his own anti-Hitler newspaper, *Der Gerade Weg (The Right Way* or *The Straight Path)* by the mid-1920s. One of the peaks of Gerlich's mounting hatred of Hitler was *Der Gerade Weg*'s sensational attack against him on July 17, 1932. Gerlich's paper featured a racially provocative photo composite image that aimed to assassinate Hitler's character. It suggested that Hitler had married a black woman. Headlining this "wedding" picture were provocative words that asked: "Does Hitler Have Mongolian Blood?"

At the heart and soul of Hitler's political creed stood the ideal of racial purity. Above all else, German or so-called Aryan blood must be kept vital and strong. Taking this ideology to be the fraud it was, Gerlich went for the jugular by spreading the impression that Hitler, the champion of "pure blood," was not only a lying hypocrite but an aspiring German leader whose character and political ambitions were rotten to the core.

No one went further than Gerlich to state publicly what others may have suspected: namely, that Hitler's appearance was scarcely like the Nordic ideal about which he could wax so eloquent. In the article that Gerlich wrote to accompany the photo montage and its scathing head-line, he brilliantly used satire to argue, in particular, that Hitler's nose could not stand the scrutiny of the "racial science" that Nazism advo-cated. Putting Hitler's nose on trial, Gerlich's article concluded that Hitler miserably failed his own racial test. Gerlich's attack on Hitler's physiognomy,[20] moreover, went more than skin deep. Persistently using the Nazis' own imagery against Hitler, Gerlich contended ironically that there could be nothing truly German about Hitler because "blood," according to Nazi ideology, was a matter of spirit as well as the key ele-ment in physical life. In Gerlich's view, Hitler's theories and political practices—despotic and corrupt at once—were profoundly at odds with the highest Germanic ideals.

Hitler was not pleased. Soon after Gerlich's article appeared, Nazis attacked the journalist's apartment building. Undaunted, Gerlich used the next week's issue of *Der Gerade Weg* to press the issue further. On July 24, 1932, he made clear that his lampoon had in no way been an endorsement of the Nazi racism he found so abhorrent. His point had not been to put Hitler on the low end of a racial hierarchy. To the con-

---

20 **physiognomy:** facial features that supposedly determine ethnic origin.

trary, he stated, all people are essentially equal because their souls are "bestowed on them by God." Furthermore, invoking religious tradition, Gerlich insisted that no man or woman could be racially inferior because "we are all descendants of one father and one mother, children of Adam and Eve."

Gerlich wanted his fellow Germans to understand that Hitler's way was neither the right way nor the German way. As 1932 wore on, Gerlich and the other anti-Hitler journalists had some reason to hope. Although the Nazis had achieved their high-water mark in freely contested national elections by winning 37.3 percent of the popular vote (230 seats in the *Reichstag*[21]) on July 31, 1932, their popularity declined during the next elections. On November 6, 1932, they received 33.1 percent of the popular vote and their Reichstag seats declined to 196. But overall the political tide was running with Hitler more than against him, and the anti-Hitler journalists could not stem it. Still, Fritz Gerlich did not give up.

On March 9, 1933, more than five weeks after Hitler took power, Gerlich prepared to publish yet another anti-Hitler attack in *Der Gerade Weg*. Perhaps he wanted to make new charges about Hitler's role in the untimely death of Geli Raubal. Perhaps he intended to arouse suspicion that the Nazis themselves—not Communists, as the Nazis claimed—had torched the Reichstag building on February 27, an action that Hitler used to convince the German president, Paul von Hindenburg, to issue the "Presidential Decree for the Protection of People and State."

Its emergency measures, which remained in place throughout the Nazi period, suspended freedom of speech, press, and assembly; eliminated freedom from invasion of privacy; and abolished freedom from house search without warrant. These measures also made distribution of politically unacceptable material a treasonous crime punishable by death.

Apparently a last-ditch effort to derail Hitler, the contents of Gerlich's March 9 report remain unknown because on that day, as journalist Ron Rosenbaum aptly summarizes the situation: "Storm Troopers burst into Gerlich's newspaper office, ripped his last story from the presses, beat him senseless, and dragged him off to Dachau." Gerlich was imprisoned in the German concentration camp for more

---

21 *Reichstag:* parliament.

than a year. Then, his wife got the message that the Nazis had killed the journalist who had seen through them all. The notice contained no words, just his steel-rimmed, blood-spattered spectacles. ∾

A watchtower at Dachau concentration camp, where Fritz Gerlich spent the last year of his life.

Responding to Cluster One

How Could the Holocaust Happen?

Thinking Skill ANALYZING

1. From the selections in this cluster and what you already know, **analyze** the roots of the holocaust. (*Analyze* means to break something into parts and study each part.) You might use a chart such as the one below to record your analysis.

Selection	Your Analysis
The Ball	Friedrich didn't break the shop window, but the owner blamed him because he was a Jew. Many Germans hated Jews, so it was easy for Hitler to blame them for the bad economy and other major problems.

2. Why do you think so many young Germans were attracted to the Hitler Youth movement? Use examples from the selection(s) to support your answer.

3. In the poems "Family Album" and "Anti-Semitic Demonstration" which lines did you find most powerful? Explain.

4. Compare the poem "Crystal Night" with the autobiographical essay "Broken Glass, Broken Lives." What did you learn about *Kristallnacht* (Crystal Night) from the poem that you did not learn from the essay?

5. Analyze the structure the author chose in "Fritz Gerlich's Spectacles." Evaluate whether the structure makes points clear, convincing, and engaging.

Writing Activity: Analyzing the Roots of the Holocaust

Analyze the selections in this cluster, looking for specific attitudes and/or actions that would allow the Nazis to take power and to commit the injustices that led to the Holocaust. The chart from question one above can help you organize your ideas. Present your analysis in the format of your choice. You might present a timeline or chart or discuss your opinions in an essay.

A Strong Analysis

- states the purpose for the analysis
- demonstrates careful examination of each part of the topic
- supports each point with evidence
- organizes information clearly
- ends with a summary of the ideas presented

CLUSTER TWO

How Were Victims Oppresssed?

Thinking Skill   COMPARING/CONTRASTING

A Spring Morning

IDA FINK

During the night there was a pouring rain, and in the morning when the first trucks drove across the bridge, the foaming Gniezna River[1] was the dirty-yellow color of beer. At least that's how it was described by a man who was crossing this bridge—a first-class reinforced concrete bridge—with his wife and child for the last time in his life. The former secretary of the former town council heard these words with his own ears: he was standing right near the bridge and watching the Sunday procession attentively, full of concern and curiosity. As the possessor of an Aryan great-grandmother he could stand there calmly and watch them in peace. Thanks to him and to people like him, there have survived to this day shreds of sentences, echoes of final laments, shadows of the sighs of the participants in the *marches funèbres*,[2] so common in those times.

"Listen to this," said the former secretary of the former town council, sitting with his friends in the restaurant at the railroad station—it was all over by then. "Listen to this: Here's a man facing death, and all he can think about is beer. I was speechless. And besides, how could he say that? I made a point of looking at it, the water was like water, just a little dirtier."

"Maybe the guy was just thirsty, you know?" the owner of the bar suggested, while he filled four large mugs until the foam ran over. The

---

1 **Gniezna:** river in Poland.

2 ***marches funèbres:*** funeral marches; When the Germans invaded Russia, they began killing any Jcews in occupied territory. Special Action Forces would march Jews, Communists, and Gypsies to the edge of town and shoot them. The victims were usually buried in mass graves.

clock above the bar rattled and struck twelve. It was already quiet and empty in town. The rain had stopped and the sun had broken through the white puffs of clouds. The sizzle of frying meat could be heard from the kitchen. On Sunday, dinner should be as early as possible. It was clear that the SS shared that opinion. At twelve o'clock the ground in the meadow near the forest was trampled and dug up like a fresh wound. But all around it was quiet. Not even a bird called out.

When the first trucks rode across the bridge over the surging Gniezna, it was five in the morning and it was still completely dark, yet Aron could easily make out a dozen or so canvas-covered trucks. That night he must have slept soundly, deaf to everything, since he hadn't heard the rumbling of the trucks as they descended from the hills into the little town in the valley. As a rule, the rumbling of a single truck was enough to alert him in his sleep; today, the warning signals had failed him. Later, when he was already on his way, he remembered that he had been dreaming about a persistent fly, a buzzing fly, and he realized that the buzzing was the sound of the trucks riding along the high road above his house—the last house when one left the town, the first when one entered it.

They were close now, and with horrifying detachment he realized that his threshold would be the first they crossed. "In a few minutes," he thought, and slowly walked over to the bed to wake his wife and child.

The woman was no longer asleep—he met her gaze immediately, and was surprised at how large her eyes were. But the child was lying there peacefully, deep in sleep. He sat down on the edge of the bed, which sagged under his weight. He was still robust, though no longer so healthy looking as he used to be. Now he was pale and gray, and in that pallor and grayness was the mark of hunger and poverty. And terror, too, no doubt.

He sat on the dirty bedding, which hadn't been washed for a long time, and the child lay there quietly, round and large and rosy as an apple from sleep. Outside, in the street, the motors had fallen silent; it was as quiet as if poppy seeds had been sprinkled over everything.

"Mela," he whispered, "is this a dream?"

"You're not dreaming, Aron. Don't just sit there. Put something on, we'll go down to the storeroom. There's a stack of split wood there, we can hide behind it."

"The storeroom. What a joke. If I thought we could hide in the storeroom we'd have been there long ago. In the storeroom or in here, it'll make no difference."

He wanted to stand up and walk over to the window, but he was so heavy he couldn't. The darkness was already lifting. He wondered, are they waiting until it gets light? Why is it so quiet? Why doesn't it begin?

"Aron," the woman said.

Again her large eyes surprised him, and lying there on the bed in her clothing—she hadn't undressed for the night—she seemed younger, slimmer, different. Almost the way she was when he first met her, so many years ago. He stretched out his hand and timidly, gently, stroked hers. She wasn't surprised, although as a rule he was stingy with caresses, but neither did she smile. She took his hand and squeezed it firmly. He tried to look at her, but he turned away, for something strange was happening inside him. He was breathing more and more rapidly, and he knew that in a moment these rapid breaths would turn into sobs.

"If we had known," the woman said softly, "we wouldn't have had her. But how could we have known? Smarter people didn't know. She'll forgive us, Aron, won't she?"

He didn't answer. He was afraid of this rapid breathing; he wanted only to shut his eyes, put his fingers in his ears, and wait.

"Won't she, Aron?" she repeated.

Then it occurred to him that there wasn't much time left and that he had to answer quickly, that he had to answer everything and say everything that he wanted to say.

"We couldn't know," he said. "No, we wouldn't have had her, that's clear. I remember, you came to me and said, 'I'm going to have a child, maybe I should go to a doctor.' But I wanted a child, I wanted one. And I said, 'Don't be afraid, we'll manage it somehow. I won't be any worse than a young father.' I wanted her."

"If only we had a hiding place," she whispered, "if we had a hiding place everything would be different. Maybe we should hide in the wardrobe, or under the bed. No . . . it's better to just sit here."

"A shelter is often just a shelter, and not a salvation. Do you remember how they took the Goldmans? All of them, the whole family. And they had a good bunker."

"They took the Goldmans, but other people managed to hide. If only we had a cellar here . . . "

"Mela," he said suddenly, "I have always loved you very much, and if you only knew—"

But he didn't finish, because the child woke up. The little girl sat there in bed, warm and sticky from her child's sleep, and rosy all over. Serious, unsmiling, she studied her parents' faces.

"Are those trucks coming for us, Papa?" she asked, and he could no longer hold back his tears. The child knew! Five years old! The age for teddy bears and blocks. Why did we have her? She'll never go to school, she'll never love. Another minute or two . . .

"Hush, darling," the woman answered, "lie still, as still as can be, like a mouse."

"So they won't hear?"

"So they won't hear."

"If they hear us, they'll kill us," said the child, and wrapped the quilt around herself so that only the tip of her nose stuck out.

How bright her eyes are, my God! Five years old! They should be shining at the thought of games, of fun. Five! She knows, and she's waiting just like us.

"Mela," he whispered, so the child wouldn't hear, "let's hide her. She's little, she'll fit in the coal box. She's little, but she'll understand. We'll cover her with wood chips."

"No, don't torture yourself, Aron. It wouldn't help. And what would become of her then? Who would she go to? Who would take her? It will all end the same way, if not now, then the next time. It'll be easier for her with us. Do you hear them?"

He heard them clearly and he knew: time was up. He wasn't afraid. His fear left him, his hands stopped trembling. He stood there, large and solid—breathing as if he were carrying an enormous weight.

It was turning gray outside the window. Night was slipping away, though what was this new day but night, the blackest of black nights, cruel, and filled with torment.

They were walking in the direction of the railroad station, through the town, which had been washed clean by the night's pouring rain and was as quiet and peaceful as it always was on a Sunday morning.

They walked without speaking, already stripped of everything human. Even despair was mute; it lay like a death mask, frozen and silent, on the face of the crowd.

The man and his wife and child walked along the edge of the road by the sidewalk; he was carrying the little girl in his arms. The child was quiet; she looked around solemnly, with both arms wrapped around her father's neck. The man and his wife no longer spoke. They had said their last words in the house, when the door crashed open, kicked in by the boot of an SS-man. He had said then to the child, "Don't be afraid, I'll carry you in my arms." And to his wife he said, "Don't cry. Let's be calm. Let's be strong and endure this with dignity." Then they left the house for their last journey.

For three hours they stood in the square surrounded by a heavy escort. They didn't say one word. It was almost as if they had lost the power of speech. They were mute, they were deaf and blind. Once, a terrible feeling of regret tore through him when he remembered the dream, that buzzing fly, and he understood that he had overslept his life. But this, too, passed quickly; it was no longer important, it couldn't change anything. At ten o'clock they set out. His legs were tired, his hands were numb, but he didn't put the child down, not even for a minute. He knew it was only an hour or so till they reached the fields near the station—the flat green pastures, which had recently become the mass grave of the murdered. He also recalled that years ago he used to meet Mela there, before they were husband and wife. In the evenings there was usually a strong wind, and it smelled of thyme.

The child in his arms felt heavier and heavier, but not because of her weight. He turned his head slightly and brushed the little girl's cheek with his lips. A soft, warm cheek. In an hour, or two . . .

Suddenly his heart began to pound, and his temples were drenched with sweat.

He bent towards the child again, seeking the strength that flowed from her silky, warm, young body. He still didn't know what he would do, but he did know that he had to find some chink through which he could push his child back into the world of the living. Suddenly he was thinking very fast. He was surprised to see that the trees had turned green overnight and that the river had risen; it was flowing noisily, turbulently, eddying and churning; on that quiet spring morning, it was the only sign of nature's revolt. "The water is the color of beer," he said aloud, to no one in particular. He was gathering up the colors and smells of the world that he was losing forever. Hearing his voice, the child squirmed and looked him in the eye.

"Don't be afraid," he whispered, "do what Papa tells you. Over there, near the church, there are a lot of people, they are going to pray. They are standing on the sidewalk and in the yard in front of the church. When we get there, I'm going to put you down on the ground. You're little, no one will notice you. Then you'll ask somebody to take you to Marcysia, the milkmaid, outside of town. She'll take you in. Or maybe one of those people will take you home. Do you understand what Papa said?"

The little girl looked stunned; still, he knew she had understood.

"You'll wait for us. We'll come back after the war. From the camp," he added. "That's how it has to be, darling. It has to be this way," he whispered quickly, distractedly. "That's what you'll do, you have to obey Papa."

Everything swam before his eyes; the image of the world grew blurry. He saw only the crowd in the churchyard. The sidewalk beside him was full of people, he was brushing against them with his sleeve. It was only a few steps to the churchyard gate; the crush of people was greatest there, and salvation most likely.

"Go straight to the church," he whispered and put the child down on the ground. He didn't look back, he didn't see where she ran, he walked on stiffly, at attention, his gaze fixed on the pale spring sky in which the white threads of a cloud floated like a spider web. He walked on, whispering a kind of prayer, beseeching God and men. He was still whispering when the air was rent by a furious shriek:

"Ein jüdisches Kind!" [3]

He was still whispering when the sound of a shot cracked like a stone hitting water. He felt his wife's fingers, trembling and sticky from sweat; she was seeking his hand like a blind woman. He heard her faint, whimpering moan. Then he fell silent and slowly turned around.

At the edge of the sidewalk lay a small, bloody rag. The smoke from the shot hung in the air—wispy, already blowing away. He walked over slowly, and those few steps seemed endless. He bent down, picked up the child, stroked the tangle of blond hair.

"Deine?" [4]

He answered loud and clear, *"Ja, meine."* [5] And then softly, to her, "Forgive me."

He stood there with the child in his arms and waited for a second shot. But all he heard was a shout and he understood that they would not kill him here, that he had to keep on walking, carrying his dead child.

"Don't be afraid, I'll carry you," he whispered. The procession moved on like a gloomy, gray river flowing out to sea. ∾

---

3 *Ein jüdisches Kind!"*: German for *a Jewish child!*

4 *"Deine?*: "Yours?."

5 *"Ja, meine."*: "Yes, mine."

The Little Boy with His Hands Up

YALA KORWIN

Your open palms raised in the air
like two white doves
frame your meager face,
your face contorted with fear,
grown old with knowledge beyond your years.
Not yet ten. Eight? Seven?
Not yet compelled to mark
with a blue star[1] on white badge
your Jewishness.

No need to brand the very young.
They will meekly follow their mothers.

You are standing apart
against the flock of women and their brood
with blank, resigned stares.
All the torments of this harassed crowd
are written on your face.
In your dark eyes—a vision of horror.
You have seen Death already
on the ghetto streets, haven't you?
Do you recognize it in the emblems
of the SS-man facing you with his camera?

Like a lost lamb you are standing
apart and forlorn beholding your own fate.

1 **blue star:** The Nazis required all Jews to wear the Star of David, a six-pointed
symbol of Judaism. Most Jews wore a yellow star, but Polish Jews wore a
blue star on a white armband.

2 **Einstein . . . Halevy:** famous Jewish people. Einstein was a physicist,
Spinoza a philosopher, and Heine and Halevy poets.

Where is your mother, little boy?
Is she the woman glancing over her shoulder
at the gunmen by the bunker's entrance?
Is it she who lovingly, though in haste,
buttoned your coat, straightened your cap,
pulled up your socks?
Is it her dreams of you, her dreams
of a future Einstein, a Spinoza,
another Heine, or Halevy[2]
they will murder soon?
Or are you orphaned already?
But, even if you still have a mother,
she won't be allowed to comfort you
in her arms.
Her tired arms loaded with useless bundles
must remain up in submission.

Alone you will march
among other lonely wretches
toward your martyrdom.

Your image will remain with us
and grow and grow
to immense proportions,
to haunt the callous world,
to accuse it, with ever stronger voice,
in the name of the million youngsters
who lie, pitiful rag-dolls,
their eyes forever closed.

Personal items collected
from gas chamber victims.

Shipment to Maidanek[1]

EPHIM FOGEL

Arrived from scattered cities, several lands,
intact from sea land, mountain land, and plain,
Item: six surgeons, slightly mangled hands,
Item: three poets, hopelessly insane,

Item: a Russian mother and her child,
the former with five gold teeth and usable shoes,
the latter with seven dresses, peasant-styled.

Item: another hundred thousand Jews.

Item: a crippled Czech with a handmade crutch.
Item: a Spaniard with a subversive laugh;
seventeen dozen Danes, nine gross of Dutch.

Total: precisely a million and a half.

They are sorted and marked—the method is up to you.
The books must be balanced, the disposition stated.
Take care that all accounts are neat and true.

Make sure that they are thoroughly cremated.

1 **Maidanek:** Polish concentration camp. Unlike most camps, it served several purposes: death camp, forced labor camp, and prison for criminals.

A Survivor Remembers

BEREK LATARUS

*Berek Latarus worked with his father in the family lumber business after
graduating from high school, buying firewood by the carload and selling it
to bakeries and factories. He could have stayed behind as a laborer when
the Germans liquidated the Lodz ghetto, but he chose to go with
his family to Auschwitz. He is the only survivor.*

When we heard the Germans were coming, everybody ran out
in the street. We saw them on their motorcycles, with the dogs
and everything, and it was kind of fun, an army comes in. Our
parents said, "Ah, we know the Germans. They're going to be the same
like it was in our war." Really, average people were not afraid. They
didn't know what was going on in the world. They were occupied with
work, with children.

THE OCCUPATION But right away the Germans burned the synagogue. Lodz
had one of the most beautiful synagogues in the world, and they burned it
to the ground. They took some Jewish people—women and men—and
hanged them in the market by the feet with the head down, to show us we
would have to be scared.

THE GHETTO They made a ghetto, strangled you around with barbed
wire. You couldn't go out, but you were afraid to escape, anyway. Where
would you go? To the Germans? Everybody was working for the Germans
in straw factories and shoe factories and clothing factories. I was deliv-
ering for the Germans, straw, food, fabrics to the clothing factories, in

trucks and by horse and buggy. For the work you'd get stamps for groceries, maybe two or three pounds potatoes a week for a whole family, one loaf of bread, some horsemeat. You couldn't live on it, and you couldn't starve on it!

People who didn't work, you used to see them swollen from not eating, and they just died on the sidewalks. In the ghetto you knew everybody, so you knew friends who died. There used to be mass funerals.

There was a curfew, and rules where you could not assemble. On every Jewish holiday, the Germans sent people to concentration camps. The first that went were the educated people—doctors, lawyers. Then they went for the older people who were not able to work. In 1940 the Germans threw the children out of the window onto trucks. I saw them do it.

In Poland people used to save gold and diamonds, that was their security. The Kripo, they knew which Jewish family had gold or diamonds. After my father died in 1942, I was three times in the Kripo. The one in charge used to be in the same business as my father, so he knew. I had to take everything my father had hidden and give it to him. Otherwise they would have killed me.

DEPORTATION The day they liquidated the ghetto they told us to take whatever we can carry with us. And then we came to the boxcars, and they didn't let us take nothing. Chased us into the boxcars and closed the doors. We were riding with no food, no water, two or three days. One of the stations we stopped at, they opened the door for fresh air and some of the Polish people tried to give us water.

Nobody knew where people were sent. We thought they shipped them out to Germany or somewhere else in Poland, for work. Nobody knew about Auschwitz, or concentration camps, or the ovens.

AUSCHWITZ In Auschwitz, the first thing, they separated women from men. Then you took off your clothes to take a shower, and when you walked out of the shower they gave you a pair of wooden shoes and the uniform with the stripes—pants and a short jacket.

In the barracks you were sleeping on a burlap sack with straw inside, on a bunk, until four or five o'clock in the morning. Then they woke you up so they could count you and select you for work. Our barracks was close to the crematorium, and we could smell that smoke from the chimneys.

In the morning they were supposed to give you coffee, but the kapo, he either liked you or he would just pour it on the floor and tell you to wipe it up. They gave you a piece of bread that's supposed to last you two or three days. If you ate it up, the other two days you starved for it, but when you didn't eat it, the next one stole it from you. I saw with my own eyes, sons stealing food from their own fathers. People don't realize what hunger means.

In one camp I was working in the kitchen so I had enough to eat, but in other camps I was like anybody else. One time I stole a bread and they took me to shoot me, but a non-Jewish guy from Cracow, he was my friend, and he ran and took me away from the Germans! This non-Jew was on good terms with the S.S., he used to smuggle them cigarettes, and we called him the "Jewish father" because he was sticking up for us all the time.

To survive you had to be lucky, keep yourself clean, stay well. We had just the one uniform, never washed, never cleaned, but you could wash with cold water sometimes. Some people who were sick, hungry, they got so depressed they didn't take care of themselves. People who got sick, you didn't see them any more. I never got sick.

To survive you also had to always look like you were working, like you were digging, or something. Some people couldn't work, and then you heard the guns. And you had to use your head. People who were smoking used to sell their soup for a cigarette. These people didn't survive. And some people were so religious they used to go during the day in a corner to pray. When somebody from the S.S. caught them praying, they were through, too.

THE TRANSPORT From Auschwitz we were sent to Regensburg, locked in boxcars for days. There were people in the boxcars so hungry they couldn't control themselves. They would bite the flesh out from dead people, eat the flesh of other people who were already dead.

By Regensburg we worked on the railroad to clean up every morning from the Allied bombing. One day we saw planes coming. Our guards ran away, and the bombs fell where they hid. They got killed and we were free! I ran with two friends, and we were hiding in a cemetery. An old woman gave us food and clothes and told us, "Go away," but civilian Germans surrounded us, and took us back to camp.

Later our camp was walking for weeks to another part of Germany. I was still with people from my town, relatives, friends, people I grew up with. My three uncles, they were very strong guys, but they got sick and couldn't walk any more. They shot all three. Everybody was waiting for their turn. I really didn't think about surviving; I thought more that I was going to be dead.

We were walking through this little town, Laufen, in May 1945 when some farmers came running out on the highway, saying, "The war is over!"

LIBERATION There was an army camp not far from there, and it became a D.P. camp.[1] Then later we moved into a house, four of us guys. We opened a Jewish Center and I was president. HIAS helped us, and UNRRA [United Nations Relief and Rehabilitation Agency].

Scale model of victims on their way to the gas chambers at Auschwitz. The Holocaust Museum, Washington, D.C.

People started leaving to look for relatives. I knew my own family went to the crematorium, but I looked for aunts and uncles, a relation. I couldn't find anybody. One of the guys I lived with, his sister came looking for him, and we got married in 1947. In 1948 our daughter was born. My brother-in-law and I opened a fabric store, buy from the factory and sell, from one town to another in Germany and Austria. My wife had a sister who came to the United States, so that's why we came.

LOOKING BACK I was really bitter about the Germans after the war, but you change. You have good people, you have bad people, that doesn't do any good. I believe in God now.

When my children were growing up, there were nights I couldn't sleep. I was still in Auschwitz and could still see everything. It was heartbreaking, and I used to cry. I really couldn't talk to my children about it, but my children and my grandchildren, they said to me, "Why don't you tell me?" Now I feel it should be talked about. ∾

1 **D. P.**: displaced persons. After they were liberated, prisoners were housed in camps for displaced persons. Over 300,000 Jews were homeless; others did not want to return to their former homes. A Jewish group smuggled almost 200,000 survivors to Palestine.

Responding to Cluster Two

How Were Victims Oppressed?

Thinking Skill COMPARING/CONTRASTING

1. The process of dehumanization was a tool used by the Nazis in an attempt to crush the spirit of victims and to protect the perpetrators from guilt. Define *dehumanization*, using a dictionary if necessary. Find examples of this process in any three of the selections in this cluster. Be prepared to discuss your answers.

2. **Compare** the fictional "A Spring Morning" to the oral history "A Survivor Remembers." In your opinion, which piece more powerfully portrays the horror of the Holocaust? Explain your response.

3. The poem "The Little Boy with His Hands Up" is based on the image on page 63. **Compare** the photo and the poem. Discuss whether or not the poem effectively reflects the event pictured in the photo.

4. Which of the selections you've read would be most likely to convince a bystander to help a victim? Give reasons for your answers.

Writing Activity: Contrasting War and Everyday Life

Part of the nightmarish quality of the Holocaust is the contrast between incredible evil occurring in the midst of normal everyday life. Choose one of the selections in this cluster and write a brief essay demonstrating this contrast. As prewriting, you might want to chart the contrasts in an organizer such as the one below.

"A SPRING MORNING"

Evil	Everyday Events
Child shot and killed	People going to church

A Strong Comparison/Contrast

- states the purpose for the comparison
- is organized in one of two ways:
  a) lists all similarities between two things; then lists all differences
  b) lists similarities and differences item by item
- summarizes the similarities and differences

CLUSTER THREE

WAS THERE RESISTANCE?

Thinking Skill   GENERALIZING

Saving the Children

FRIEDA SINGER

to Gizelle Hersh

They had taken away
her hair
her shoes
her name a bluish numeral
under the skin[1]
her gender denied
in a sea of men
yet something of her
as she was remained.

In the barracks
where work makes one free[2]
she learned to stand
motionless from five to ten
for *Zeile Appell*[3]
camouflaging her skin where
blemishes meant selection to the left,[4]
urging her sisters
who refused
the moldy soup
the sawdust bread
that to eat was to resist
to eat, even to eat
the pain.

1 **bluish numeral . . . :** tattoo. Jewish prisoners were given an identity number to dehumanize them.

2 **work makes one free:** translation of the motto above the gates of Auschwitz, *Arbeit Macht Frei*.

3 *Zeile Appell:* roll call.

4 **selection:** sorting process. Healthy prisoners went to the right; the young, the old, and the ill were sent to their deaths.

To eat, even when
the throat gagged
from the disinfecting stench;

to eat, even with
swollen ears
and frozen feet
in cubicles too narrow
to stand or sleep
where one worn blanket
was assigned to cover ten;

to swallow
even the teeth marks
of the snarling kapo guard
doubling back upon them
the injuries from above.

To remember always
that first day
when a flick of the wrist
sent her to the right
her parents to the left.

Mother, where are you,
twelve year old Katya would scream
night after night.
At sixteen, more adult than child,
she had promised
to care for the children
the promise that kept her
and them alive.

Rescue in Denmark

Harold Flender

*When the Nazis planned to arrest the Danish Jews, a German official named
Georg Duckwitz gave warning. Word spread quickly. Ordinary Danes hid Jews
in homes, shops, barns, and convents. The Germans were able to capture
only 484 Jews. More than 7,000 were smuggled to safety in Sweden.*

One escape route was organized by Dr. Karl Henry Køster, who
recruited most of the staff of Bispebjerg Hospital to the rescue effort.

Dr. Køster's most important opportunity to thwart the Germans came
on October 7, 1943. On that day, Ole Secher, one of his medical
students, paid him an unexpected visit.

"Our student group has discovered forty Jews hiding out in the woods
south of Copenhagen," said Secher. "We've made arrangements to have
them taken by truck to some fishing boats tomorrow night, but there are
quite a few Germans in the woods and we need a better place for the
truck to make the pickup. Would it be possible for you to hide them here
in the hospital for a couple of hours until the truck arrives to get
them?"

"I'm sure we could," replied Dr. Køster. "But how would you get
them here?"

"We've thought of that," replied Secher. "We'll stage a mock funeral,
dress the Jews in black, have them carry flowers while following a hearse
through Copenhagen to the cemetery on the hospital grounds."

"But the cemetery is small," commented Køster. "You can't have the
truck pick them up there. It'll be too conspicuous. We often have

Danish fishermen help Jewish refugees
escape to Sweden, 1943.

Germans, including the Gestapo, on the hospital grounds. I suggest we keep them in the chapel until the truck comes for them."

"Perfect," said Secher. "We'll have the phony funeral procession go right from the front gate to the chapel. That's an excellent suggestion. You can expect the forty Jews here first thing tomorrow morning."

At 8:30 A.M. Køster received a telephone call from a distressed gate-keeper. "A whole bunch of Danes have just come in for a funeral," he said.

"Well," asked Køster, "what's so unusual about that?"

"We never have funerals here so early in the morning."

"Sometimes we do," said Køster.

"In the thirty-five years I've been gatekeeper we've never had a funeral here so early in the morning."

"But these are unusual times," said Dr. Køster. "We're under the German occupation."

"But nobody told me there was going to be a funeral here this morning," said the gatekeeper. "Why was I not informed?"

"I forgot to tell you," said Køster. "I had an emergency operation to perform last night and it must have slipped my mind. Yes, I meant to tell you to expect about forty mourners."

"There aren't forty," said the gatekeeper. "There are more than a hundred and forty!"

"Are you sure?"

"Yes."

"Well," said Dr. Køster, "let them through."

He ran down to the gate to see for himself, and there, sure enough, were at least 140 "mourners." Included among them was his student Ole Secher. Dr. Køster joined the funeral procession, marching next to Secher.

"What happened?"

"Some of them told others," said Secher, "and I couldn't very well tell any of them not to come. So here they are."

Slowly the funeral entourage made its way up the tree-lined path to the chapel on top of the hospital grounds.

"Have you made arrangements for transportation for the additional refugees?" asked Køster.

"No," said Secher. "There's only one truck for the forty refugees."

"Perhaps it can make two more trips."

"No," said Secher. "The arrangements we've made with the fishermen are for only forty refugees."

Over 140 refugees entered the chapel. A couple of hours later a canvas-covered lorry entered the hospital grounds and drove up to the chapel. Forty refugees chosen at random were loaded inside the truck. As the last of the forty climbed on board, Dr. Køster noticed a Gestapo car pull up several hundred yards down the road.

"What'll we do?" he asked.

"What can we do?" replied Secher. "We'll have to hope they got there too late to notice anything." He signaled the driver to proceed.

As the truck pulled away, the canvas flap at the rear of the truck was suddenly pulled back and one of the refugee children, waving his hand, yelled, "Bye, bye, everybody!" He then let the flap close.

The Gestapo car started following the truck.

Dr. Alan Gammeltoft, who had been working with Ole Secher in rescuing the refugees, said, "They might not have seen the refugees getting into the truck from the chapel, but they must have seen the little boy waving good-bye."

"Maybe they didn't," said Secher. "They were still down the road when it happened."

"Then why are they following the truck now?" asked Dr. Gammeltoft. "We had better not take any chances. I'm going to get into my automobile and ram the Gestapo car. I'll try to make it look like an accident."

He jumped into his automobile and gave pursuit. Outside the hospital grounds, just as Dr. Gammeltoft was about to slam his foot down on the accelerator and crash into the Gestapo car, it turned down another road.

Returning to the chapel with the good news, Dr. Gammeltoft found Dr. Køster and Ole Secher engrossed in trying to decide what to do with the one hundred refugees who had been left behind. They could not remain in the chapel. What was particularly distressing was that there was no way of knowing how long they would have to be kept on the hospital grounds. Obviously it would take at least a day or two for arrangements to be made to have them taken to Sweden. Meanwhile, there were the questions of housing and food. The doctors decided that the department of the hospital with the most room was the psychiatric building. It was also one of the least likely sections to be searched by the Germans. In groups of two and three, with spacings of at least five minutes between each group, the refugees were led from the chapel to the psychiatric building.

The following morning, Dr. Køster received another telephone call from the gatekeeper. "More mourners."

It came as a complete surprise to Dr. Køster. "How many?"

"At least two hundred."

Dr. Køster wondered what the devil was wrong with Secher. Where could they possibly put two hundred additional refugees? There was no more room in the psychiatric building. After the new arrivals were in the chapel, Dr. Køster approached Head Nurse Signe Jansen.

"Do you think you might find room for some of these refugees in the nurses' quarters?"

"I'll speak to my nurses," said Nurse Jansen.

A little while later Nurse Jansen returned to Dr. Køster with a huge batch of keys. "The nurses are willing," she said. "Here are the keys to thirty apartments in the nurses' quarters. Some of the nurses will stay in their apartments with the refugees, sleeping on the couch or on the floor. Others will double up with other nurses."

The two hundred new refugees were taken to the nurses' quarters. Later that afternoon Ole Secher showed up. He knew nothing about the new arrivals. "It must have spread by word of mouth that Bispebjerg is a good place to hide," he said.

"That means we can expect even more refugees."

"I suppose so," replied Secher.

That evening, before curfew, an additional hundred refugees showed up. Dr. Køster was no longer distressed. Bispebjerg was a good place for the refugees to hide. They could sleep in the nurses' quarters and be fed from the hospital kitchen. All that remained were the arrangements that had to be made with fishermen to take the refugees across to Sweden. . . .

In a matter of days, Bispebjerg Hospital became one of the most important collection points for the refugees, with virtually the entire medical staff cooperating to save the lives of their fellow countrymen. The nurses put 130 apartments at the disposal of the refugees, and the only time Head Nurse Signe Jansen had complaints from her staff was when there were not enough refugees in the apartments. The nurses vied with each other in trying to help the Jews.

▲   ▲   ▲

Toward the end of October, the Germans increased their vigil at Bispebjerg Hospital, and the rescue of the Danish Jews became more difficult. Occasionally, the Germans would raid the operating theater of Bispebjerg Hospital, and when a doctor was found performing surgery on a Jewish patient, the Germans would machine-gun to death patient, doctor and everyone else in the room assisting the operation. One of Dr. Køster's closest friends, an outstanding surgeon, was killed in this fashion.

▲ ▲ ▲

[One night Dr. Køster's wife warned him that Gestapo officers were waiting for him at their apartment.] Dr. Køster went straight to the home of his friend Peter Heering, owner of the well-known Cherry Heering factory outside of Copenhagen. He remained in hiding there for ten days, after which he was smuggled to Sweden aboard a schooner. In Stockholm, Køster contacted the British Embassy and offered his services to them as a doctor. The British Embassy arranged for him to get to London, like Niels Bohr,[1] in the bomb bay of an R.A.F. "Mosquito."[2]

While serving as a medical officer with the British armed forces, Dr. Køster was among the first to enter the Bergen Belsen concentration camp in 1945. What he saw there convinced him more graphically than anything else possibly could that he had been right in helping to save the lives of the two thousand Danish Jews.

▲ ▲ ▲

"Because the entire medical profession stood together as a single unit in opposition to anti-Semitism, our efforts in behalf of our countrymen of the Jewish faith were that much easier," said Dr. Køster. "We knew that the Germans couldn't arrest all of us." ∾

---

1 **Niels Bohr:** famous physicist who traveled to Sweden to persuade officials there to accept Jewish refugees from Denmark.

2 **R.A.F. "Mosquito":** British fighter plane.

Members of the White Rose (from left) Hans Scholl, Sophie Scholl, and Christoph Probst, l942.

The White Rose: Long Live Freedom

JACOB G. HORNBERGER

Small pamphlets urging Germans to resist the "abominable tyrant"
Adolf Hitler began appearing in 1942. They were distributed by a student
movement called The White Rose. Though the original members of the
White Rose were executed for treason, an organization by that
name continues their work for freedom.

The date was February 22, 1943. Hans Scholl and his sister Sophie, along with their best friend, Christoph Probst, were scheduled to be executed by Nazi officials that afternoon. The prison guards were so impressed with the calm and bravery of the prisoners in the face of impending death that they violated regulations by permitting them to meet together one last time. Hans, a medical student at the University of Munich, was 24. Sophie, a student, was 21. Christoph, a medical student, was 22.

This is the story of The White Rose. It is a lesson in dissent. It is a tale of courage—of principle—of honor. It is detailed in three books—*The White Rose* (1970) by Inge Scholl, *A Noble Treason* (1979) by Richard Hanser, and *An Honourable Defeat* (1994) by Anton Gill.

Hans and Sophie Scholl were German teenagers in the 1930s. Like other young Germans, they enthusiastically joined the Hitler Youth. They believed that Adolf Hitler was leading Germany and the German people back to greatness.

Their parents were not so enthusiastic. Their father—Robert Scholl—told his children that Hitler and the Nazis were leading Germany down a road of destruction. Later—in 1942—he would serve time in a Nazi prison for telling his secretary: "The war! It is already lost. This Hitler is God's scourge on mankind, and if the war doesn't end soon the Russians will be sitting in Berlin."

Gradually, Hans and Sophie began realizing that their father was right. They concluded that, in the name of freedom and the greater good of the German nation, Hitler and the Nazis were enslaving and destroying the German people.

They also knew that open dissent was impossible in Nazi Germany, especially after the start of World War II. Most Germans took the traditional position—that once war breaks out, it is the duty of the citizen to support the troops by supporting the government.

But Hans and Sophie Scholl believed differently. They believed that it was the duty of a citizen, even in times of war, to stand up against an evil regime, especially when it is sending hundreds of thousands of its citizens to their deaths.

The Scholl siblings began sharing their feelings with a few of their friends—Christoph Probst, Alexander Schmorell, Willi Graf—as well as with Kurt Huber, their psychology and philosophy professor.

One day in 1942, copies of a leaflet entitled "The White Rose" suddenly appeared at the University of Munich. The leaflet contained an anonymous essay that said that the Nazi system had slowly imprisoned the German people and was now destroying them. The Nazi regime had turned evil. It was time, the essay said, for Germans to rise up and resist the tyranny of their own government. At the bottom of the essay, the following request appeared: "Please make as many copies of this leaflet as you can and distribute them."

The leaflet caused a tremendous stir among the student body. It was the first time that internal dissent against the Nazi regime had surfaced in Germany. The essay had been secretly written and distributed by Hans Scholl and his friends.

Another leaflet appeared soon afterward. And then another. And another. Ultimately, there were six leaflets published and distributed by Hans and Sophie Scholl and their friends—four under the title "The White Rose" and two under the title "Leaflets of the Resistance." Their publication took place periodically between 1942 and 1943—interrupted for a few months when Hans and his friends were temporarily sent to the Eastern Front to fight against the Russians.

The members of The White Rose, of course, had to act cautiously. The Nazi regime maintained an iron grip over German society. Internal dissent was quickly and efficiently smashed by the Gestapo. Hans and Sophie Scholl and their friends knew what would happen to them if they were caught.

People began receiving copies of the leaflets in the mail. Students at the University of Hamburg began copying and distributing them. Copies began turning up in different parts of Germany and Austria.

Moreover, as Hanser points out, the members of The White Rose did not limit themselves to leaflets. Graffiti began appearing in large letters on streets and buildings all over Munich: "Down with Hitler! . . . Hitler the Mass Murderer!" and "Freihart! . . . Freihart! . . . Freedom! . . . Freedom!"

The Gestapo was driven into a frenzy. It knew that the authors were having to procure large quantities of paper, envelopes, and postage. It knew that they were using a duplicating machine. But despite the Gestapo's best efforts, it was unable to catch the perpetrators.

One day—February 18, 1943—Hans' and Sophie's luck ran out. They were caught leaving pamphlets at the University of Munich and were arrested. A search disclosed evidence of Christoph Probst's participation, and he too was soon arrested. The three of them were indicted for treason.

On February 22—four days after their arrest—their trial began. The presiding judge, Roland Freisler, chief justice of the People's Court of the Greater German Reich, had been sent from Berlin. Hanser writes:

> He conducted the trial as if the future of the Reich were indeed at stake. He roared denunciations of the accused as if he were not the judge but the prosecutor. He behaved alternately like an actor ranting through an over-written role in an implausible melodrama and a Grand Inquisitor calling down eternal damnation on the heads of the three irredeemable heretics before him. . . . No witnesses were called, since the defendants had admitted everything. The proceedings consisted almost entirely of Roland Freisler's denunciation and abuse, punctuated from time to time by half-hearted offerings from the court-appointed defense attorneys, one of whom summed up his case with the observation, "I can only say *fiat justitia*. Let justice be done." By which he meant: Let the accused get what they deserve.

Freisler and the other accusers could not understand what had happened to these German youths. After all, they all came from nice German families. They all had attended German schools. They had been members of the Hitler Youth. How could they have turned out to be traitors? What had so twisted and warped their minds?

Sophie Scholl shocked everyone in the courtroom when she remarked to Freisler: "Somebody, after all, had to make a start. What we wrote and said is also believed by many others. They just don't dare to express themselves as we did." Later in the proceedings, she said to him: "You know the war is lost. Why don't you have the courage to face it?"

In the middle of the trial, Robert and Magdalene Scholl tried to enter the courtroom. Magdalene said to the guard: "But I'm the mother of two of the accused." The guard responded: "You should have brought them up better." Robert Scholl forced his way into the courtroom and told the court that he was there to defend his children. He was seized and forcibly escorted outside. The entire courtroom heard him shout: "One day there will be another kind of justice! One day they will go down in history!"

Robert Freisler pronounced his judgment on the three defendants: Guilty of treason. Their sentence: Death.

They were escorted back to Stadelheim prison, where the guards permitted Hans and Sophie to have one last visit with their parents. Hans met with them first, and then Sophie. Hanser writes:

> His eyes were clear and steady and he showed no sign of dejection or despair. He thanked his parents again for the love and warmth they had given him and he asked them to convey his affection and regard to a number of friends, whom he named. Here, for a moment, tears threatened, and he turned away to spare his parents the pain of seeing them. Facing them again, his shoulders were back and he smiled . . .
>
> Then a woman prison guard brought in Sophie. . . . Her mother tentatively offered her some candy, which Hans had declined. "Gladly," said Sophie, taking it. "After all, I haven't had any lunch!" She, too, looked somehow smaller, as if drawn together, but her face was clear and her smile was fresh and unforced, with something in it that her parents read as triumph. "Sophie, Sophie," her mother murmured, as if to herself. "To think you'll never be coming through the door again!" Sophie's smile was gentle. "Ah, Mother," she said. "Those few little years. . . ." Sophie Scholl looked at her parents and was strong in her pride and certainty. "We took everything upon ourselves," she said. "What we did will cause waves." Her mother spoke again: "Sophie," she said softly, "remember Jesus." "Yes," replied Sophie earnestly, almost commandingly, "but you, too." She left them, her parents, Robert and Magdalene Scholl, with her face still lit by the smile they loved so well and would never see again. She was perfectly composed as she was led away. Robert Mohr [a Gestapo official], who had

come out to the prison on business of his own, saw her in her cell immediately afterwards, and she was crying. It was the first time Robert Mohr had seen her in tears, and she apologized. "I have just said good-bye to my parents," she said. "You understand . . . " She had not cried before her parents. For them she had smiled.

No relatives visited Christoph Probst. His wife, who had just had their third child, was in the hospital. Neither she nor any members of his family even knew that he was on trial or that he had been sentenced to death. While his faith in God had always been deep and unwavering, he had never committed to a certain faith. On the eve of his death, a Catholic priest admitted him into the church *in articulo mortis*—at the point of death. "Now," he said, "my death will be easy and joyful."

That afternoon, the prison guards permitted Hans, Sophie, and Christoph to have one last visit together. Sophie was then led to the guillotine. One observer described her as she walked to her death: "Without turning a hair, without flinching." Christoph Probst was next. Hans Scholl was last; just before he was beheaded, Hans cried out: "Long live freedom!"

Unfortunately, they were not the last to die. The Gestapo's investigation was relentless. Later tried and executed were Alex Schmorell (age 25), Willi Graf (age 25), and Kurt Huber (age 49). Students at the University of Hamburg were either executed or sent to concentration camps.

Today, every German knows the story of The White Rose. A square at the University of Munich is named after Hans and Sophie Scholl. And there are streets, squares, and schools all over Germany named for the members of The White Rose. The German movie *The White Rose* is now found in video stores in Germany and the United States.

Richard Hanser sums up the story of The White Rose:

In the vogue words of the time, the Scholls and their friends represented the "other" Germany, the land of poets and thinkers, in contrast to the Germany that was reverting to barbarism and trying to take the world with it. What they were and what they did would have been "other" in any society at any time. What they did transcended the easy division of good-German/bad-German and lifted them above the nationalism of time-bound events. Their actions made them enduring symbols of the struggle, universal and timeless, for the freedom of the human spirit wherever and whenever it is threatened. ∾

The Warsaw Ghetto Uprising

REUBEN AINSZTEIN

The single greatest act of Jewish resistance during the war was the defense of the Warsaw Ghetto. The ghetto was the walled area of the city where Jews were confined. On April 19, 1943, German troops begin to liquidate the ghetto. Resistance fighters held them off for three weeks. Eighteen-year-old Jacob Smakowski, who fought to avenge the deaths of his mother and sister, wrote this account of the fighting. Portions of his diary are reprinted in The Warsaw Ghetto Revolt *by Reuben Ainsztein.*

It must have been the 28th of April. In Muranów Square the Germans ordered captured Jews to take off all their clothes, then searched their clothes, took their money and gold, ordered them to dress and marched them off. When night came we attempted to reach the "Aryan" side, but when about one hundred of us tried to get over the Muranowska-Pokorna wall, the Germans opened fire at us from where the Poles had been removed. About fifty of our group were killed and the survivors retreated.

Later the Germans made a breach in the wall where we had tried to escape and placed there ten gendarmes[1] armed with rifles, who fired at every Jew attempting to get out. The following morning Pika[2] noticed fifteen gendarmes come through the breach in the wall and make for our house, because during the previous night they had observed that we had

---

1 **gendarmes:** policemen with military training.
2 **Pika:** leader of the Mila Street fighters.

been firing at them from it. Pika, in his SS uniform, advanced towards them and said in a loud voice: *"Ja, ja, hier sind Juden da."* ("Yes, yes, there are Jews here.") They saluted and Pika led them into the courtyard to show them where the Jews were. We were on the ground floor and when the gendarmes reached the middle of the courtyard, we opened fire and killed the fifteen of them.

Later we raised over our corner house, No. 42 Nalewki Street and No. 17 Muranowska Street, two flags, a white-red one and a white-blue one, to show that we were not giving up, that we were insurgents. Poles watched through binoculars how we fired at the Germans and the Germans fired at us. Next to the flags on the fourth floor we placed a bomb, which we concealed under rubble and stones, so that those who attempted to take down the flags would be blown to pieces. We made the flags out of table-cloths; I sewed them together in our bunker. The Germans drove up in tanks. When they approached our house, we opened fire and withdrew to No. 40, Nalewki Street and from there to No. 38, where the Braun workshops were, and there we hid on the stair-case of the fourth floor. That was our last chance. We reckoned that as soon as the Germans approached we would open fire and withdraw. Should it prove impossible, we would shoot ourselves, for each of us kept his last bullet for himself. Some had cyanide for this purpose.

A number of our lads withdrew to No. 15, Muranowska Street. We saw the tanks stop outside No. 42, from where nobody fired at them. Behind the tanks came Germans and Ukrainians. The Ukrainians went up to the fourth floor and approached our flags. Suddenly there was a terrific explosion, the wall collapsed and buried the invaders. The same night we learnt that a dozen or more of them had been killed. The flags were fixed to a wall and next to it we had dug a hole, so that in order to reach the flags the Germans would be forced to step where the bomb was buried. And this is what happened.

After our success we moved to No. 6, Walowa Street. There we were reached by a boy who had fled from the bunker under No. 42, Nalewki Street. He told us that the Germans had dragged out of the bunker more than forty Jews and shot them in the courtyard. Several managed to escape through a back exit. They did it in retaliation for our flags. In our group was a lad whom we called "The Yellow Mellon." He proposed that we mine our gateway and kill the Germans who tried to come near us. We placed mines on both sides of the gateway, then we barricaded it and then placed dynamite above it. As soon as the Germans approached, we lit the fuse. The

Warsaw Ghetto inhabitants are rounded up for transit to concentration camps, 1943.

mine exploded and the group of Germans was killed. The explosion was so great that the gateway became impassable.

The Aktion[3] was then in its second week. Two weeks passed since the outbreak of the uprising and the Germans had still not managed to get through. For us it was a convenient defensive position, for opposite us there were also ruins. Unable to get at us through No. 6, Walowa Street, they tried through No. 32, Swietojerska Street. We let them come through there because we had placed a mine and when their tank rolled over it, the tank and its crew were blown up. The Ukrainians then opened up. We retreated to No. 6, Walowa Street, but they succeeded in taking alive a number of our lads.

[Eventually, the resistance fighters were forced to leave the ghetto. Some escaped to the forests, where they continued to fight until the Red Army liberated Warsaw in January 1945.

When the battle was over, 7,000 Jews had been killed in the fighting, 6,000 had burned to death in their hideouts, and 56,000 were transported to the gas chambers at Treblinka.]

Perhaps the military significance of the Warsaw Ghetto Uprising has been best summed up by the Polish General Jerzy Kirchmayer, the historian of the Warsaw Uprising of 1944.

The blows delivered by the Jewish fighters hurt badly the prestige of General Stroop's "heroes," who, although armed to the teeth, were forced to bring in tanks, artillery and planes against insurgents who were almost completely devoid of arms . . . .

The Warsaw ghetto fell after a heroic fight, but the idea of armed struggle, in the name of which the insurgents had died, reached beyond the walls, survived and endured until victory. ◠

---

3 **Aktion:** German attack on the ghetto.

APPEAL OF THE JEWISH FIGHTING ORGANIZATION TO THE POLISH POPULATION

POLES, CITIZENS, SOLDIERS OF FREEDOM!

Through the din of German cannon destroying our homes, the homes of our mothers, wives and children; through the noise of their machine-guns, seized by us in the fight against the German police and S.S. men; through the smoke of the fires and the blood of those murdered in the Warsaw Ghetto, we convey greetings to you.

We are aware that you have been witnessing with anguish and tears of compassion, with amazement and breathless anticipation, the war we have been waging against the occupation forces during the past few days.

But you can have seen and will see every doorstep in the ghetto becoming a stronghold and remaining a fortress until the end. All of us may perish in the fight but we shall never surrender. We, as well as you, are burning with the desire to punish the enemy for all his crimes, with a desire for vengeance. It is a fight for our freedom as well as yours.

It is a fight for our human dignity and social and national honor, as well as yours.

We shall take vengeance for Oswiecim, Treblinka, Belzec and Maidanek!

Long live the comradeship of arms and blood of fighting Poland! Long live freedom!

Death to the murderous and criminal occupation forces!

Let us wage the life and death struggle against the German occupation forces until the very end!

Jewish Fighting Organization
April 23, 1943

Using leaflets and flyers, Jewish fighters pleaded for help from Polish citizens outside the ghetto. However, few Poles were willing to resist the German troops.

RESPONDING TO CLUSTER THREE

WAS THERE RESISTANCE?

Thinking Skill GENERALIZING

1. Many people believe that no citizens or Holocaust victims resisted the Nazis. Others think that individuals were powerless against the Nazis' organized brutality. Use information from this cluster and what you already know to generate a list of strategies people used to resist the Nazis.

2. In Latvia, Lithuania, and Poland, nine out of ten Jews were killed. However, in Denmark, nine out of ten Jews were saved. **Generalize** about the conditions that might explain why so many Jews were saved in Denmark.

3. In your opinion, were the members of The White Rose foolish or heroic? Use evidence from the selection "The White Rose" to explain your answer.

4. The "Appeal of the Jewish Fighting Organization to the Polish Population" contains persuasive language and punctuation designed to convince others to join their cause. To understand these persuasive techniques, rewrite the appeal, making it as neutral as possible.

Writing Activity: Generalizing About Holocaust Resistance

Write a generalization about resistance during the Holocaust. A *generalization* is a conclusion drawn from several different pieces of information. You might generalize about why people chose to resist, the most effective way to resist, or whether ordinary people had any chance to resist. Then support your generalization with quotations or specific examples from the selections you have read.

A Strong Generalization

- is based on facts
- draws conclusions from several sources
- avoids blanket statements
- avoids universal terms such as *all, always,* and *never*
- uses specific language and examples

CLUSTER FOUR

Why Should We Remember?
Thinking Skill SYNTHESIZING

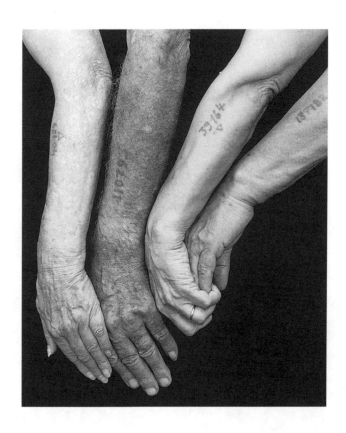

An American soldier distributes cigarettes to prisoners within Dachau.

Letter from Dachau

1st Lt. William J. Cowling

*The first American soldier to enter Dachau describes his experience in
a letter to his family. Over 30,000 prisoners and 100 SS guards remained
in the camp when it was surrendered to Lt. Cowling.*

28 April [1945]

Dear Folks:

Boy, oh boy, am I having a heck of a time trying to find time to write. We are
really moving. My days have been consisting of getting up between 6:30
and 7:30, eating, throwing my stuff in a Jeep and taking off. When visit-
ing the regiments and sometimes the battalions and then heading for a
new CP,[1] by the time we get into the new CP and set up it is 11 o'clock at
night or later, and I am so tired I just hit the sack, so I really haven't had
much time to write. I received the fruit cake the other day and boy was it
good. That package contained all the right things. I have lost my chap-
stick and my lips were chapped so it really came in handy.

Well, I was interrupted at this point and it is now the 30th of April and
the very first minute I have had to write. Since I started this letter I
have had the most, I suppose you would say, exciting, horrible and at the
same time wonderful experience I have had ever or probably ever will
have. When I tell it to you you probably won't believe all the details. I
knew when I heard such stories back in the States I never believed them

1 **CP:** command post.

and now even after seeing with my own eyes, it is hard for me to believe it. Well, to go on with the story, as you know we have been moving very rapidly and oftentimes the boss and I get into the towns just about the same time the front line troops do. Yesterday we started out to locate a company and a unit advancing down a road. Enroute we learned from civilians and two newspaper people that just off the main road was a concentration camp of Dachau, oldest largest and most notorious camp in Germany. These newspaper people were going up to see the Camp so we decided to go up too.

We ride in a Jeep with a guard out ahead of the boys and we were several hundred yards ahead as we approached the Camp. The first thing we came to was a railroad track leading out of the Camp with a lot of open box cars on it. As we crossed the track and looked back into the cars the most horrible sight I have ever seen (up to that time) met my eyes. The cars were loaded with dead bodies. Most of them were naked and all of them skin and bones. Honest, their legs and arms were only a couple of inches around and they had no buttocks at all. Many of the bodies had bullet holes in the back of their heads. It made us sick at our stomach and so mad we could do nothing but clench our fists. I couldn't even talk. We then moved on towards the Camp and my Jeep was still several hundred yards ahead. As we approached the main gate a German officer and a civilian wearing an International Red Cross band and carrying a white flag came out. We immediately filed out and I was just hoping he would make a funny move so I could hit the trigger of my tommy gun. He didn't, however, and when he arrived abreast of us he asked for an American officer. I informed him he was talking to one and he said he wished to surrender the Camp to me.

About that time the General[2] arrived and got the story from the German Lieutenant (that the Camp was still manned by German guards who were armed but had orders not to shoot at us but only to keep the prisoners in check). Well, about that time somebody started shooting from over on our left flank and [we] ducked but made the Germans stand in front of us. Finally the fire let up and we sent one of the guards back for a company of infantry. The newspaper people said they were going on into Camp, and I got permission to go on with them with my guard, leaving the others with the General. We went through one gate and spotted some Germans in a

---

2 **the General:** General Linden, Assistant Division Commander of the 42nd Division. Lt. Cowling was the general's aide.

tower. I hollered in German for them to come to me and they did. I sent them back to the guards and General and got on the front of the newspaper people's Jeep and headed for the gate.

A man lay dead just in front of the gate. A bullet through his head. One of the Germans we had taken lifted him out of the way and we dismounted and went through the gate into a large cement square—about 800 squares surrounded by low black barracks and the whole works enclosed by barbed wire. When we entered the gate not a soul was in sight. Then suddenly people (if you could call them that) came from all directions. They were dirty, starved skeletons with torn tattered clothes and they screamed and hollered and cried. They ran up and grabbed us—myself and the newspaper people—and kissed our hands and feet, and all of them tried to touch us. They grabbed us and tossed us into the air screaming at the top of their lungs. I finally managed to pull myself free and get to the gate and shut it so they could not get out. Then I felt something brush my shoulder and I turned to the left of the two block houses guarding the gate to find a white flag fluttering square in my face and on the end of it inside the house eight Germans.

I looked around the house and entered. I got the same question, are you an American officer, and said Yes. They turned over their arms, pistols and rifles to me and I told them to sit tight. I then went back outside and sent my driver to get the Jeep. Then I went back into the Germans and took their arms and sent the pistols to my Jeep. (I gave all away but two.) When I came back out the General was there and the people inside the enclosure were all in the large square shouting and crying. Then a terrible thing happened. Some of them in their frenzy charged the barbed wire fence to get out and embrace us and touch us. Immediately they were killed by an electric charge running through the fence. I personally saw three die that way. Our troops arrived about that time and took the rest of the guards, Germans (who during all this time had remained in the towers around the prison). A number of them and I sincerely regret that I took the eight prisoners that I did after a trip through Camp which I shall describe in a minute.

Well, the General attempted to get the thing organized, and an American Major who had been held in the Camp since September came out and we set him up as head of the prisoners. He soon picked me to quiet the prisoners down and explain to them that they must stay in the Camp until we could get them deloused, and proper food and medical care. Several newspaper people arrived about that time and wanted to go through the Camp,

Reunion of U.S. troops and Jewish prisoners one year after the liberation of Dachau, 1946.

so we took them through with a guide furnished by the prisoners. The first thing we came to were piles and piles of clothing, shoes, pants, shirts, coats, etc. Then we went into a room with a table with flowers on it and some soap and towels. Another door with the word showers led off of this and upon going through this room it appeared to be a shower room but instead of water, gas came out and in two minutes the people were dead. Next we went next door to four large ovens where they cremated the dead. Then we were taken to piles of dead. There were from two to fifty people in a pile all naked, starved and dead. There must have been about 1,000 dead in all.

Then we went through a building where fifty men were guarded in a room the size of your kitchen. There were hundreds of typhus cases and all through the Camp men cheered us and tried to touch us. Incidentally many of the dead and living showed signs of horrible beatings and torture. It is unbelievable how any human can treat others as they were treated. One wasted little man came up and touched my sleeve and kissed my hand. He spoke perfect English and I asked him if he were American. He said no, Jewish, and that he was one of the very few left—that thousands had been killed. He had been there six years. He was twenty-eight years old and looked to be sixty years old. The Germans I took prisoner are very fortunate they were taken before I saw the Camp. I will never take another German prisoner armed or unarmed. How can they expect to do what they have done and simply say I quit and go scot-free. I know now why our men kick and abuse the German prisoners. They are not fit to live.

Well, that's my story. A day I will never forget. It will get a lot of publicity and you may see General Linden's name connected with Dachau, but you can know in your own minds that it was your son who was the first American soldier to enter the famous Camp of Dachau. I know that sounds like bragging but I only say it because it is true and I know that the story won't come out that way but several thousand prisoners will remember me. Incidentally there were 32,000 prisoners in the Camp. They were Polish, Jewish, French, German and even American. Well, I must stop now. The next time I write I hope I can say that I got my first German and I don't mean prisoner.

Owe the Germans a lot now.

Incidentally, you're griping about my going to the South Pacific. I have only been in the Army a couple of years. Some of these people were in the hell hole of Dachau for years. If I spend ten years in the Army during war I will never go through what those people go through. Even if I were killed, I would be lucky compared to those people. So if you still feel the jitters, remember the people of Dachau and think how lucky I am no matter what happens.

We will write and I will give you the rest of the story when I get home.

Love, Bill

Reunions

BERNARD GOTFRYD

It was May, 1945, and the war was over. For two days I had been in Linz, Austria, alone, living in constant anxiety over the fate of my family. I was afraid to think about who was still alive. Every day I crisscrossed the city of Linz, hoping to find a trace of something familiar, a clue, a contact of some kind. I wasn't even sure if I still remembered the faces of my brother and sister or my parents; I wasn't sure that they would recognize me if we were to meet.

Nightmarish images were always before my eyes, keeping me awake at night. I had nothing left, not even a picture, to prove that I had once belonged to a family. I didn't know who I was; I had doubts about my own name. I remembered only my prisoner number, as if it were engraved on my brain.

Who am I, I kept asking myself, and what am I doing here? I looked and searched but kept running away from myself.

Soon I moved on to Salzburg, about seventy-five miles from Linz, to get away from an imaginary SS man I thought was out to kill me. In my mind he looked like Horst Gartner, whose parents had invited me to stay at their house. Salzburg was no better, only somewhat larger than Linz; registrations and inquiries, survivors looking for relatives, lists of survivors on walls, and notices in different languages were everywhere. Everybody was looking for somebody else, but no one, it seemed, was looking for me. I found no familiar names, not even that of a neighbor. Slowly I was coming to terms with the fact that, at the age of twenty, I was alone in the world.

Warsaw in ruins. 1945.

One early morning, while walking near the railway station in search of a photo shop, I heard someone calling from the other side of the street. The call came again; it was my name. At first I couldn't identify with it; when I finally turned I saw a stocky young man of medium height with a full, round face and closely cropped hair. Who was he? He had the face of a stranger, and his voice was unfamiliar. He was wearing a pair of baggy pants and a striped shirt with rolled-up sleeves; he carried a small suitcase with reinforced metal corners.

When I stopped he started running toward me, yelling my name at the top of his lungs. When he realized I wasn't responding he dropped the suitcase, grabbed me by my shoulders, and shook me hard, as if trying to wake me from a sleep.

"I'm your brother, don't you recognize me?" he yelled. He had heard that I was in Austria and had traveled for two days from Stuttgart, sitting on top of a coal car, to look for me. "Are you all right?" he asked. "Or is there something wrong with you?" We hugged, and he nearly squashed me; he was strong.

"I just couldn't recognize you," I said, fighting back my tears. "I didn't think I would ever see you again. It's almost unreal how different you look; you've gained a lot of weight, your hair is short. God, you look like a different person. How could I have recognized you?"

"I had a bad case of typhoid," he said, "and since I got well I haven't been able to stop eating. I've been liberated since April and have been living on a farm with some friends. Recently we slaughtered a pig; you can imagine how well we eat.

"You probably don't know that Father was shot," my brother went on to say. He had witnessed Father's execution. Matter-of-factly he described the whole scene to me. "I begged the SS man to let Father go," he told me, "but he threatened to shoot me, too, and I think he would have if I hadn't stepped back into the ranks. I remember him very well. I even know his name and where he came from. It was terrible and frightening. I can't forget it."

For a split second I remembered my father throwing the egg to me at the Szkolna camp. I remembered his tears when the SS guard hit him with a stick for doing so; every time I thought of my father there were tears; still, I couldn't cry. It seemed impossible that I was talking to my brother.

An Austrian woman with big, sad eyes and a knapsack strapped to her back stopped to watch us; she stood a few feet away shaking her head. I didn't think she knew what was happening or who we were, but when we started walking away she looked back over her shoulder, still shaking her head. I heard her say *"Wie traurig"*—how sad—before we disappeared around the corner.

My brother had heard rumors from survivors who traveled across Europe looking for their families that our sister Hanka was alive and looking for us in Poland.

We stayed together for a while, but toward the end of the summer we parted again. My brother remained in Germany; I went to Poland via Prague to search for our sister.

It was difficult and lonely journey that took me back to a country I dreaded, a journey full of strange and unpredictable encounters. I traveled in the backs of trucks or in unheated trains, standing up for hours on steps or in open freight cars, often enough in the rain. The Nazis had robbed the country of everything; there were few scheduled trains or buses. The same hateful faces greeted me wherever I went. The same resentment came through all of their eyes; I could see they were wondering why I had come back.

Cold winds and rain blew incessantly across the Polish landscape, turning it into one huge mud pie. I traveled from one city to another searching for my sister, only to find that she had eluded me each time by leaving a day or two before I arrived. I kept moving from place to place, hoping to catch up with her; in Lodz a Polish friend of the family, Mr. S., gave me some money my parents had left with him for safekeeping and told me that my sister had left for Stettin on her way to the west.

The following day I hitched a ride on a truck going toward the German frontier. As soon as I climbed in the back of the truck it started raining, so I slipped under the tarpaulin and stretched out on a pile of potato sacks behind some wooden crates. It was late in the evening when the truck approached the first intersection; it slowed down. I heard part of a conversation with the driver, and soon I saw two armed men in uniforms climb in the back. They settled themselves directly across from where I was lying; even in the dark something told me that they weren't friendly.

I was correct in my assessment; when the truck started moving again I heard the two men talking. They complained about what a wasted day it had been; they hadn't found a single Jew. I broke out in a cold sweat. What if they discovered me? Suppose they decided to lift the tarpaulin? That would be the end of me. What could I possibly tell them? About my time in the camps, and how much I longed to get back to my home town and find my people? How could they understand me if they were out to kill me? Only several days before I had heard someone talk about armed bands of Polish nationalists who were organizing pogroms against Jewish survivors. These people were no better than the Nazis; I hated the thought that I might have survived the camps to meet my fate at the hands of Polish hooligans.[1]

My stomach felt as if it were tied into a knot. I tried not to move or even breathe. If only I could shrink to the size of an insect or change into an earthworm! Kafka's *Metamorphosis*[2] came to my mind, and I prayed for a miracle.

Suddenly I felt like sneezing. I was terrified; instinctively I pressed my nose against the edge of a crate and stopped breathing. It worked. I hoped I wouldn't have to repeat the trick; next time I might not be as lucky. I could still hear my traveling companions making threats against the Jews.

It must have been well past midnight. There was no moon, and the rain was coming down incessantly. One side of my face kept getting wet, and drops of water were rolling down my neck behind my shirt collar. It was getting cold; I began to shiver. From time to time the truck would zigzag to avoid a pothole, and the smaller load at the tail of the truck would slide and bounce against the crates, pushing them against my legs.

The two men continued to discuss their exploits and their frustrations. The one with the hoarser voice was recounting how he and some of his friends had recently executed a whole Jewish family who had survived the war in an underground shelter in the woods. He described the episode in vivid detail. It was a bloodcurdling story. The two men sat at the edge of the truck with their feet hanging down and with their backs to me. With one eye I was able to make out their silhouetted torsos against the misty night.

Some hours passed, and finally I heard a knocking above my head, at the driver's cab window. At the next intersection the truck came to a stop, and the two men got off. I watched them jump across the ditch and disappear into the woods. I felt as though I had been liberated for a second time.

I didn't know how far it was to Stettin, but I didn't care. I crawled from under the tarpaulin and looked out. It had stopped raining, and the haze was lifting. There was a strong aroma of rotting leaves mixed with cow

---

1 Five hundred Jews were killed by anti-Semites after they returned to Poland.

2 **Metamorphosis:** story in which a young man changes into a cockroach.

manure. At the side of the road I could see faint outlines of bare trees with twisted branches, as if multitudes of crisscrossing arms were reaching for the sky. Some distance away I could make out farm huts with thatched roofs; the flickering lights of kerosene lamps reflected against their tiny windows, making them look like squatting monsters with burning eyes.

It was a sad and desolate landscape. Here and there were clusters of birch and pine trees. The white birch trunks seemed to be moving across the fields like ghosts, as though they were racing with the truck. From time to time I could hear the driver curse in Polish or sing old Jewish tunes. I was astounded. How did he know Jewish tunes? He had a husky voice and a rich vocabulary of four-letter words with which he seemed to amuse himself.

It was dawn when the truck reached the gates of the city. When it came to a full stop the driver clambered out of the cab, yawning and stretching, to announce our arrival in the city of Stettin. This was as far as he was going.

"This is it," he said. "Last stop." I jumped off the truck holding on to my knapsack. Every muscle in my body ached. I walked over to the driver. He was a husky blond man, perhaps in his thirties. "How do you happen to know Jewish tunes?" I asked him carefully.

"Oh, well," he answered, "it's a long story, but since you ask I'll tell you, I happen to be Jewish. Simple as that. So are you, right? I didn't even have a good look at you, but my antennae tell me you must be one, too," he said, winking at me.

"How could I deny it?" I asked him, and the two of us laughed. It felt so much safer now that the trip was over.

"By the way," I said, "do you happen to know who those two armed men were you had on your truck?"

"I don't know them personally, but I imagine they were members of some political faction; fanatics. There are quite a few of them around, and they always hitch rides; it could be dangerous for me to refuse them. Don't forget, they're armed, and I'm not."

"I was frightened when they got on the truck," I admitted. "They were really dangerous."

"Frankly, I had no idea you were Jewish," he said. "I never had a good look at you before you got on the truck. But don't be afraid, it's over. God protected you."

"You look so Polish, so Christian," I said. "I would have never taken you for a Jew."

"That is exactly what saved me," he said. "My looks. But who are you, and where are you going?" he asked. I told him briefly where I came from and for whom I was looking. "My God," he exclaimed, "it must have been real tough for you. You should be happy to be alive and have a sister. Look at me; I'm the only one from my family left alive. I know what it is like to be left alone."

When I tried to reward him for his trouble he wouldn't accept any money. I offered him my last pack of Chesterfields, but he would only take a few cigarettes. He drove me closer to the center of the city and let me off in front of a teahouse surrounded by ruins. "This is the only place in Stettin where you can get some food. Good luck. I hope you find her," he said, smiling and shaking my hand.

I was in a strange city in which only a few buildings remained standing. It was still early. The teahouse was open, however; I could smell freshly baked bread, and the aroma reminded me of my hunger. I hadn't eaten since I got on the truck in Lodz almost twelve hours before. In the teahouse marble tables stood on massive wrought-iron stands; a long marble counter adorned with brass fixtures, a reminder of better times, ran the length of the room. On the wall hung a small Polish flag.

A young woman was filling orders behind the counter, and a teenager with a blond ponytail was waiting on tables. They didn't have much to offer; only hot tea and buttered rolls or bread. For me that fare was a treat. I sat there warming my hands on a tall glass full of steaming tea, feeling the warmth travel all the way down to my

Warsaw in ruins. 1945.

frozen toes. The place began to fill up. People were drifting in, settling in at the tables, dragging metal chairs noisily over the marble floor. I noticed a young man enter the teahouse. He wore a creased raincoat tied with a wide leather belt and carried a knapsack. He looked around as if searching for someone, then proceeded directly toward my table, where there was an empty chair. "Is it all right if I join you?" he asked.

"Please do; I haven't talked to a soul in days," I answered.

"My name is Moshe, Moshe Feingold. I'm a survivor," he introduced himself, shaking my hand rather vigorously. He pulled out the chair across from me and quickly sat down, dropping his knapsack under the table next to mine. I told him my name, and he leaned forward, coming closer to me, as if he had difficulty hearing.

"I think you must be a survivor," Moshe said in a low voice, looking at me suspiciously. "Yes, I am," I answered. "Now that our hair is still short, our clothing fits badly, and we look hungry, lost, and frightened, it must be easy to tell," I said.

"You're quite right," Moshe said, biting into his buttered roll. He was thin, and his eyes were dark and intense. When he talked his head kept turning like a radar dish, left to right, right to left. His short, curly hair was growing in in a very odd shape; the curls were connecting and pressing on each other, as if fighting for space. We sat there exchanging stories, ordering more and more tea. As far as he knew, his entire family had disappeared.

"I crisscrossed Poland, I went to see every camp that ever existed, and all I found were piles of ashes. Poland is one huge cemetery. What else is left?" he asked. "I come from Otwock, not far from Warsaw. There is not a single Jew left in the town. I got married one week before the war started. I had a wife and a little son. My son would have been four years old by now. My parents, my wife's parents, and the rest of the family were shipped to Treblinka. This much I found out."

I felt bad for him and didn't think it was appropriate for me to talk about my losses. Moshe was on his way to the west, he told me, to join some friends who were getting ready to emigrate to Palestine. We wished each other luck; a few hours into the morning he left.

I got up and went over to the counter to buy some more rolls, but before I had a chance to place my order the young woman behind the counter asked me excitedly, "Do you happen to have a relative named Hanka? I don't know her last name. You look just like her, the same mouth and eyes, the same face. She's my neighbor. She lives right around the corner, on the second floor to the right. I know her. She usually comes here for her rolls. I'm surprised she didn't show up yet this morning. I noticed the strong resemblance as soon as you came in, but then I got busy, and I lost track of you."

"I'm her brother," I answered, my knees shaking. "I've been looking for her everywhere for weeks."

"Please sit down and have some more tea," she suggested. "You must be starved. All this traveling in such bad weather." I thanked her and told her I had already eaten well, paid my check, and ran outside.

It was still early when I knocked at my sister's apartment. A young woman dressed in a long robe opened the door and instantly threw her arms around me.

"How did you find me? This is a miracle. I've been looking for you all over Poland," I heard her say into my shoulder. I couldn't speak. There were no tears, only sadness, and when we hugged a strange feeling came over me. It was as if something inside me was asking me why I was alive while so many others weren't. It pressed and nagged at me, bringing back images of those who were gone. Should I tell my sister immediately what had happened to our father? Or should I wait? I had a feeling that she already knew, that she, too, must have been wondering if I knew about Father.

I wanted to tell my sister how happy I was to find her, but I couldn't find the words. It all seemed abstract, hardly believable. What was one supposed to talk about at such moments? There was no point in recalling the tragic events; it was simply good to be alive, and to be together. Over the next few days we talked in length about many different things but never mentioned the war, nor the camps, as if it had never taken place, as if the six years had just dropped out of the calendar and disappeared. I was getting used to the idea that I was free, no longer alone, and that there were others like myself, roaming, searching, and wandering.

About ten days after my arrival my sister left Stettin, heading west to join our brother, and I set out in search of Alexandra, my wartime underground contact. I planned to rejoin my family as soon as I found her.[3] ∾

3 **contact:** Alexandra recruited the narrator into the resistance movement. She did not survive the war.

Entrance to the main camp at Auschwitz. The slogan *Arbeit Macht Frei* means "Work Makes One Free."

Return to Auschwitz

KITTY HART

As a Polish teenager, Kitty Hart survived the Lublin ghetto and eighteen months in the concentration camp at Auschwitz. In 1978, she returned to the camp with her son David. There she made the award-winning film Return to Auschwitz. *A friend urged her to "write a book, before it's all forgotten." This selection is taken from Hart's book, which has the same title as her film.*

You see grass. But I don't see any grass. I see mud, just a sea of mud. And you think it's cold? With your four or five layers of clothing on a bright crisp day like this, you feel the cold? Well, imagine people here or out beyond that fence working when it snowed, when it rained, when it was hot or cold, with one layer of clothing. The same layer and no change of clothing unless you were a skilled organizer.[1] And you couldn't take those stinking rags off or they'd be stolen immediately.

Look at me daring to walk along the *Lagerstrasse.*[2] In my day you were not supposed to even set foot on it, let alone walk along it. I close my eyes and there they are, those women, *Kapos*[3] and the rest of them, strutting up and down. It was forbidden for scum like me to venture near the edge of that trench or peer down into it.

I open my eyes, and there's nobody. Open my eyes and see grass. Close my eyes and see mud.

1 **organizer:** prisoner who could find scarce items, such as spoons and clothing.
2 *Lagerstrasse*: main road through camp.
3 *Kapos*: prisoners chosen to lead work parties.

Here it is, the gate between the two sections of the camp which I had to get through to visit my mother. And there are the electrified fences. Don't go too close. The watch-towers still look down. There must still be guns in there, trained on you.

I belong here. I knew I ought never to have come back, because it has proved I've never been away. The past I see is more real than the tidy pretence they have put in its place. The noises are as loud as they ever were: the screams, the shouts, the curses, the lash of whips and thud of truncheons, the ravening dogs. Here was where I received my personal education. This is my old school. Education sticks with you for the rest of your life. Whatever curriculum and discipline other people may cling to or rebel against from their schooldays, here is where my standards were established: to obey or try not to obey, to revolt against or slyly circumvent, and always, either way, to fear; standards which, no matter how distorted, can never be forgotten.

I walk on grass which was once interminable mud. Beneath the green surface the ground is still muddy. My feet sink in. It's not so much spongy as just that little bit wetter so that it squelches and threatens to suck you down and trap you there, so that you breathe faster and want to drag your feet out and escape before it's too late.

Imagine it (I can't imagine it any other way) with 100,000 people trudging through that mud, hear the plopping sound of wrenching your clog out of the mess until maybe you no longer had the strength to wrench it out . . .

In another thirty or forty years there will no longer be people like me alive, no one who can actually say, 'I've watched with my own eyes one, two, three million people go to their death.' I would like you, David, to be able to testify that your mother was here and you've been here with me, and tell your children what I've told you and shown you, that it will never be completely erased from history. I've had thirty good years. But most of the rest of my relatives, my grandmothers and aunts and my father's family and my mother's, and my school friends, were robbed of those years. The ashes of more than thirty of my relations could well be in this very place. Yet there are new cheats and liars and schemers writing that it never happened and couldn't have been true. So I must reply in these pages that it was true.

All a myth? Come and see for yourself.

I'm trying to locate Camp BI. It all looks so alien. With so many of the huts pulled down or fallen down, I can't get my bearings. Some of the stone huts are still intact, but the wooden ones have disintegrated, leaving an odd pattern of little brick chimneys and heating channels jutting up all over the place. But this stone building must be part of BI. Look at it. And just look over there. When I close my eyes again I see camps, nothing but camps. This one we're standing in was one of the smallest. Beyond it stretched the streets and terraces and factories of a city of slaves as far as the eye could see.

There's the railway line I helped to build, over there. Not that I actually laid the rails: I dug ditches and carried cement. That's why my hands aren't ladylike. And there's where they often turned the dogs loose on you.

Here. This is Block 20, one of the first of my huts. This door is where the *Blockälteste*[4] stood, and where the bread ration was doled out. Every time you went in you were issued with your bread ration, usually with a savage blow as well. And inside . . . come in and have a look . . . oh, yes, I often bought myself a place to sleep on one of those boards. Bought it with crumbs of bread, because if you didn't you were liable to end up on the floor. Look at the mud on the floor and imagine it. Look at the end of the hut, too. That's where the bucket was. Just one bucket, and you couldn't use it most of the time so you lay in your own mess and everyone else's mess. No water, only miserable scraps of food, and you were beaten all the time . . . how long do you think *you* would want to go on living?

Here's the little room of the *Blockälteste*. Here she kept her roll-call book, and here she slept, and here she had her own little stove to keep her warm.

Outside, the 'meadow' is green with grass. That's something I simply can't get used to. It was never like that when we stood for hours waiting for roll-call numbers to match up. Never like that when women collapsed and died in the mud or froze to death on the hard winter ground.

Another block, and what's this? A washroom actually attached to the hut. I never got as far as that in my Auschwitz career. Water was something you won only by bartering bread—if you could organize the surplus bread in the first place. You couldn't take it away in a container, so you had to bribe your way into some place where there was a tap, however miserable and polluted its trickle might be. I can hear it now, the negotiating and auctioning.

4 *Blockälteste*: block senior, a prisoner who helped supervise other prisoners.

'I've got a bowl of water. You can have it for two spoons of sugar.'

'I haven't got two spoons. Tell you what—I can manage one spoon, and a little bit of bread.'

'Here.' Another girl pushes her way in. 'If she doesn't want it, *I'll* give you two spoons of sugar for it.'

As for the official issue of drink, since liberation I have confirmed what many of us suspected at the time. Soup and so-called tea or coffee (the distinction was hazy) both had poison added. Prisoners working in the kitchen were supervised by S.S. women who regularly measured out a certain quantity of white powder into whatever the liquid might be. We assumed it was some sort of bromide[5] but had no way of discovering anything about its properties. I recently learned that a Polish doctor is currently engaged in research into the poison, which is called Avo. It contributed to the revolting smell of the soup, but you drank the stuff because you were desperate. And if you had no other food, you were in trouble.

In the hospital compound there was an abundance of *Lagersuppe*[6] because few of the sick could swallow their full ration. Prisoners on the staff lived on the leftovers. Mother had a lot of it before she noticed the effect it was having. Drink too much, and you couldn't think clearly all day. It gave you diarrhea, slowed down other physical movements, and left you totally confused. I am sure now it contributed to the degeneration of those who became *Muselmen*.[7]

. . . [In the camp there was] one necessary implement. Your bowl. I remember my bowl in Auschwitz was a red one. If you didn't have your bowl you didn't get your soup. If you didn't have your bowl you didn't have your toilet. And how did you wash the bowl out before you ate again? You didn't. Or you washed it out with your own urine.

Here's the toilet block. That came rather late on. Even then there were thousands of women trying to get in before roll-call. And no paper? You mean toilet paper? You must be joking.

Over here . . . this huge cart. Now I haven't thought of that for years. It used to be dragged into the camp loaded with bread rations, drawn by male Russian prisoners-of-war, the few survivors of the 20,000 exterminated just before our arrival in Auschwitz. Once the bread had been

---

5 **bromide:** drug used to calm nervousness or cause sleep.

6 *Lagersuppe:* camp soup.

7 *Muselmen:* prisoners who had given up hope.

distributed, the cart came in handy for removing corpses which lay by the roadside and outside every block.

Oh, God. This is the hospital compound. The very place where I had to help load Hanka and Genia on to the lorries.[8] Load my own friends on just when they were on their way to recovery from illness. That finished me. Really finished me mentally. Everyone went that day. Everybody. Only my mother stopped me going with them or on to the fence.[9]

Mother saved my life then and on so many occasions. We couldn't have survived without each other. There was no way of struggling through all on your own. You had to have somebody helping you, and you had to help somebody else; without some such bond there was nothing to cling to. I don't know much about the men's camp other than what I have since read in books such as the detailed and deeply moving Ota Kraus and Erich Kulka document, *The Death Factory* (and reading it can never be the same as living it for oneself), but those authors and others admit that conditions in the women's camp of Birkenau were many times worse that those the men had to suffer.

Down here is the *Kanada*[10] enclosure. Pretending to be a factory with a nice lawn outside. I close my eyes and at once the air is filled with screams; and when I open them I think that this is the dream, for the building isn't there, and there are no longer any chimneys for the smoke to pour out of.

We're walking through the birch wood now. There's the pond behind what used to be one of the crematoria. Yes, I'm getting my bearings, I can work out where it stood. And the sauna—look, it's still here, the very same one I remember. And I'm going to scratch my name and number and dates into the wall. I've never disfigured a monument before, but this time, I've just got to leave a record behind, to go along with my Auschwitz record which they must still have somewhere filed away in the camp archives.

The path along which our *Kapo* led us has to be here somewhere. So much is overgrown, but it must be here.

People from the whole of Europe were brought to this graveyard. Just remember, that's what it is: a vast graveyard. I'm looking for the white house, but I can't find a trace. Over there, across this clearing, maybe?

8 **lorries**: trucks.

9 **going on to the fence**: committing suicide by running into an electrified fence.

10 ***Kanada***: gas chamber.

Walking through these woods, that small group of us on our visits to the main camp, we saw . . . yes, here are the foundations. So that's all there is left? All that's left save for the echoes, the steady bup-bup-bup of pistols firing into the back of people's necks.

The ground's a different colour over here. Must be some pits or something. We climb up this mound, and on the other side that grey patch . . . you know what that is? I dig in with a stick, and up come sodden ashes and a piece of bone.

'Yes,' says David. As a doctor he has no doubts. 'This is human bone.'

A tiny morsel of one of the millions who perished here.

Let's invite those people who say it never happened, invite them here and ask them to explain these ashes and fragments of human bone. And the empty gas canisters they keep in Auschwitz museum—if there were no gassings, where did all those canisters come from and what were they used for? My eyes didn't play me false. I saw just that sort of container being tipped into the vent. And I heard the sounds that followed.

So many were exterminated that you had to numb yourself against any reaction. As long as there was a sea of people, death was too vast to comprehend. But acts of individual brutality still scream in my mind. A mother might be trying to pacify her child as she began to fear the worst, and then because of some other upset the S.S. would cease the pretence of calm and orderliness. An S.S. man might come and tear the child away, pick it up by its head or legs and just smash it to death in front of the mother. It was something never to be forgiven. Mother and child were condemned to death anyway: could they not be allowed to go to it quietly together? Even if there had been any impersonal logic behind the German extermination programme, even if they genuinely felt their basic policy was a stern moral necessity, then at least they could have let people

General view of the Birkenau (Auschwitz II) concentration camp. February, 1945.

go to their ordained death with dignity rather than under the torment of gratuitous brutality.

If instead of those unknown Germans[11] in Salzwedel I had met one of the S.S. men while the dagger was still in my hand, would I have used it? I'm pretty sure I would. And I'd have had no guilty conscience afterwards. ∾

Auschwitz, the largest death camp, covered 19 square miles. Located near the Polish town of Oswiecim, it had three major units: Auschwitz I; Auschwitz II, or Birkenau; and Auschwitz III, or Buna-Monowitz.

Auschwitz I was a concentration camp where the Nazis carried out medical experiments. Birkenau was a death camp; more than 1,250,000 prisoners died in its four killing centers. Its barracks, built to hold 48 horses, often held more than 800 people. Buna-Monowitz held hundreds of thousands of slave-laborers. Forty-five smaller camps nearby supplied cheap workers for German and Polish industries.

The first prisoners arrived in June 1940. The camp was liberated by Soviet troops five years later. As Allied troops neared the camp, the Nazis sent the prisoners on death marches and tried to destroy the camp and its records. Evidence of their war crimes still remained when Soviet troops entered the camp on January 27, 1945.

11 **unknown Germans:** When Salzwedel camp was liberated, Kitty and some friends found a German family hiding in a basement. Though Kitty had a knife, she could not bring herself to harm them. "If I committed murder, the S.S. . . . would have made me like them."

The Survivor

JOHN C. PINE

(After seeing "Kitty Hart: Return to Auschwitz" on Public TV)

She learned early that in order to survive
She would have to make herself
As small as possible and hide
Among the others, even if this meant
Concealing herself behind a corpse.
She learned also to appropriate
From the dead their bread
Ration and articles of clothing.
The sheer bureaucratic
Size and impersonality of the death camp
Worked to her advantage.
She survived also on animal instinct
And cunning. She knew that her elders
Thought too much about their situation.
Their fate could be read in the dazed
And vacant look on their faces.
After the inevitable selection they became
Spectral voices, disembodied hands
Between the iron bars of high windows.
Sometimes on warm spring days
When the foliage was beginning to turn green
And wildflowers were blooming in the woods,
She would sun herself within sight of the crematories
And observe the smoke rising from the chimneys,
And smell the stench of burning flesh
Which permeated the entire camp.
Almost thirty-five years later she returned
To Auschwitz-Birkenau with her son

From her home in Birmingham, England.
There was grass where before there had been only mud.
Some of the buildings had been torn down,
And the emptiness all round them
Was strange and unsettling. Nevertheless,
It soon came back to her. Unhesitatingly
She walked through the thick underbrush
To the pits which had been hastily dug
When the crematories could no longer
Dispose of people fast enough.
Many of those selected for extermination
Had been burned in these open pits—
Some of them while still alive.
Now poking in the ashes with a stick
She came upon a small fragment of bone
Bleached by the heat and cold of thirty-five years,
And gave it to her son as a memento
Of all that she had been witness to
And in memory of all those who nourished
The earth without even a whitish sliver
Of bone to be remembered by.

The Power of Light

ISAAC BASHEVIS SINGER

During World War II, after the Nazis had bombed and bombed the Warsaw ghetto, a boy and a girl were hiding in one of the ruins—David, fourteen years old, and Rebecca, thirteen.

It was winter and bitter cold outside. For weeks Rebecca had not left the dark, partially collapsed cellar that was their hiding place, but every few days David would go out to search for food. All the stores had been destroyed in the bombing, and David sometimes found stale bread, cans of food, or whatever else had been buried. Making his way through the ruins was dangerous. Sometimes bricks and mortar would fall down, and he could easily lose his way. But if he and Rebecca did not want to die from hunger, he had to take the risk.

That day was one of the coldest. Rebecca sat on the ground wrapped in all the garments she possessed; still, she could not get warm. David had left many hours before, and Rebecca listened in the darkness for the sound of his return, knowing that if he did not come back nothing remained to her but death.

Suddenly she heard heavy breathing and the sound of a bundle being dropped. David had made his way home. Rebecca could not help but cry "David!"

"Rebecca!"

In the darkness they embraced and kissed. Then David said, "Rebecca, I found a treasure."

"What kind of treasure?"

"Cheese, potatoes, dried mushrooms, and a package of candy—and I have another surprise for you."

"What surprise?"

"Later."

Both were too hungry for a long talk. Ravenously they ate the frozen potatoes, the mushrooms, and part of the cheese. They each had one piece of candy. Then Rebecca asked, "What is it now, day or night?"

"I think night has fallen," David replied. He had a wristwatch and kept track of the day and night and also of the days of the week and the month. After a while Rebecca asked again, "What is the surprise?"

"Rebecca, today is the first day of Hanukkah, and I found a candle and some matches."

"Hanukkah tonight?"

"Yes."

"Oh, my God!"

"I am going to bless the Hanukkah candle," David said.

He lit a match and there was light. Rebecca and David stared at their hiding place—bricks, pipes and the uneven ground. He lighted the candle. Rebecca blinked her eyes. For the first time in weeks she really saw David. His hair was matted and his face streaked with dirt, but his eyes shone with joy. In spite of the starvation and persecution David had grown taller, and he seemed older than his age and manly. Young as they both were, they had decided to marry if they could manage to escape from war-ridden Warsaw. As a token of their engagement, David had given Rebecca a shiny groschen[1] he found in his pocket on the day when the building where both of them lived was bombed.

Now David pronounced the benediction over the Hanukkah candle, and Rebecca said, "Amen." They had both lost their families, and they had good reason to be angry with God for sending them so many afflictions, but the light of the candle brought peace into their souls. That glimmer of light, surrounded by so many shadows, seemed to say without words: Evil has not yet taken complete dominion. A spark of hope is still left.

For some time David and Rebecca had thought about escaping Warsaw. But how? The ghetto was watched by the Nazis day and night. Each step was dangerous. Rebecca kept delaying their departure. It would be easier in the summer, she often said, but David knew that in their predicament, they had little chance of lasting until then. Somewhere in the forest there were young men and women called

---

1 **groschen:** bronze Austrian coin.

partisans[2] who fought the Nazi invaders. David wanted to reach them. Now, by the light of the Hanukkah candle, Rebecca suddenly felt renewed courage. She said, "David, let's leave."

"When?"

"When you think it's the right time," she answered.

"The right time is now," David said. "I have a plan."

For a long time David explained the details of this plan to Rebecca. It was more than risky. The Nazis had enclosed the ghetto with barbed wire and posted guards armed with machine guns on the surrounding roofs. At night searchlights lit up all possible exits from the destroyed ghetto. But in his wanderings through the ruins, David had found an opening to a sewer which he thought might lead to the other side. David told Rebecca that their chances of remaining alive were slim. They could drown in the dirty water or freeze to death. Also, the sewers were full of hungry rats. But Rebecca agreed to take the risk; to remain in the cellar for the winter would mean certain death.

When the Hanukkah light began to sputter and flicker before going out, David and Rebecca gathered their few belongings. She packed the remaining food in a kerchief, and David took his matches and a piece of lead pipe for a weapon.

In moments of great danger people become unusually courageous. David and Rebecca were soon on their way through the ruins. They came to passages so narrow they had to crawl on hands and knees. But the food they had eaten, and the joy the Hanukkah candle had awakened in them, gave the courage to continue. After some time David found the entrance to the sewer. Luckily the sewage had frozen, and it seemed that the rats had left because of the extreme cold. From time to time David and Rebecca stopped to rest and to listen. After a while they crawled on, slowly and carefully. Suddenly they stopped in their tracks. From above they could hear the clanging of a trolley car. They had reached the other side of the ghetto. All they needed now was to find a way to get out of the sewer and leave the city as quickly as possible.

Many miracles seemed to happen that Hanukkah night. Because the Nazis were afraid of enemy planes, they had ordered a complete black-out. Because of the bitter cold, there were fewer Gestapo guards. David and Rebecca managed to leave the sewer and steal out of the city with-

2 **partisan:** armed civilian or guerrilla fighter.

out being caught. At dawn they reached a forest where they were able to rest and have a bite to eat.

Even though the partisans were not very far from Warsaw, it took David and Rebecca a week to reach them. They walked at night and hid during the days—sometimes in granaries and sometimes in barns. Some peasants stealthily helped the partisans and those who were running away from the Nazis. From time to time David and Rebecca got a piece of bread, a few potatoes, a radish, or whatever the peasants could spare. In one village they encountered a Jewish partisan who had come to get food for his group. He belonged to the Haganah, an organization that sent men from Israel to rescue Jewish refugees from the Nazis in occupied Poland. This young man brought David and Rebecca to other partisans who roamed the forest. It was the last day of Hanukkah, and that evening the partisans lit eight candles. Some of them played dreidel[3] on the stump of an oak tree while others kept watch.

From the day David and Rebecca met the partisans, their life became like a tale in a storybook. They joined more and more refugees who all had but one desire—to settle in the Land of Israel. They did not always travel by train or bus. They walked. They slept in stables, in burned-out houses, and wherever they could hide from the enemy. To reach their destination, they had to cross Czechoslovakia, Hungary, and Yugoslavia. Somewhere at the seashore in Yugoslavia, in the middle of the night, a small boat manned by a Haganah crew waited for them, and all the refugees with their meager belongings were packed into it. This all happened silently and in great secrecy, because the Nazis occupied Yugoslavia.

But their dangers were far from over. Even though it was spring, the sea was stormy and the boat was too small for such a long trip. Nazi planes spied the boat and tried without success to sink it with bombs. They also feared the Nazi submarines which were lurking in the depths. There was nothing the refugees could do besides pray to God, and this time God seemed to hear their prayers, because they managed to land safely.

The Jews of Israel greeted them with a love that made them forget their suffering. They were the first refugees who had reached the Holy Land, and they were offered all the help and comfort that could be given. Rebecca and David found relatives in Israel who accepted them with

---

3 **dreidel:** game played at Hanukkah in using a wooden top, or dreidel, which has letters carved into its four sides.

open arms, and although they had become quite emaciated, they were basically healthy and recovered quickly. After some rest they were sent to a special school where foreigners were taught modern Hebrew. Both David and Rebecca were diligent students. After finishing high school, David was able to enter the academy of engineering in Haifa, and Rebecca, who excelled in languages and literature, studied in Tel Aviv—but they always met on weekends. When Rebecca was eighteen, she and David were married. They found a small house with a garden in Ramat Gan, a suburb of Tel Aviv.

I know all this because David and Rebecca told me their story on a Hanukkah evening in their house in Ramat Gan about eight years later. The Hanukkah candles were burning, and Rebecca was frying potato pancakes served with applesauce for all of us.

Menorah, a candle holder used during Hanukkah.

David and I were playing dreidel with their little son, Menahem Eliezer, named after both of his grandfathers. David told me that his large wooden dreidel was the same one the partisans had played with on that Hanukkah evening in the forest in Poland. Rebecca said to me, "If it had not been for that little candle David brought to our hiding place, we wouldn't be sitting here today. That glimmer of light awakened in us a hope and strength we didn't know we possessed. We'll give the dreidel to Menahem Eliezer when he is old enough to understand what we went through and how miraculously we were saved." ☙

RESPONDING TO CLUSTER FOUR

WHY SHOULD WE REMEMBER?

Thinking Skill SYNTHESIZING

1. Below are statements from three of the selections in this cluster. Compare the attitude toward the persecutors represented by each statement. Then explain what you think each of the speakers would want us to remember about the Holocaust.

   "I will never take another German prisoner armed or unarmed. How can they expect to do what they have done and simply say I quit and go scot-free."
   —1ST LT. WILLIAM J. COWLING

   "If instead of those unknown Germans in Salzwedel I had met one of the S.S. men while the dagger was still in my hand, would I have used it? I'm pretty sure I would. And I'd have had no guilty conscience afterwards."
   —KITTY HART

   "If it had not been for that little candle David brought to our hiding place, we wouldn't be sitting here today. That glimmer of light awakened in us a hope and strength we didn't know we possessed. We'll give the dreidel to Menahem Eliezer when he is old enough to understand what we went through and how miraculously we were saved."
   —REBECCA IN "THE POWER OF LIGHT"

2. "The Power of Light" contains powerful symbolism. In literature, a *symbol* is an object that comes to stand for a larger idea or concept. What symbols do you find in this story and what meaning does each represent?

3. "Return to Auschwitz," "The Power of Light," and "Reunions" tell the stories of several survivors of the Holocaust. Identify at least three characteristics of the survivors in these selections.

4. Many readers find descriptions of the horrors of the Holocaust profoundly disturbing. Do you think that if everyone learned of these horrors, such knowledge would prevent future holocausts from occurring? Be prepared to discuss your response.

Writing Activity: Why We Remember—A Synthesis

Compose a creative written product such as a poem, song, letter, editorial, or journal entry in which you present your feelings about why the Holocaust should be remembered and studied. You might want to consider your response to question four above.

A Strong Synthesis

- begins with a careful analysis of details
- develops into a rearrangement of material
- shares a distinctly fresh viewpoint in a personal and new way

CLUSTER FIVE

THINKING ON YOUR OWN

For the Dead and the Living

ELIE WIESEL

Elie Wiesel, a Holocaust survivor, is an author who has won the Nobel Peace Prize. This essay is adapted from the speech he gave in 1993 at the dedication of the United States Holocaust Memorial Museum in Washington, D.C.

With the exception of Israel, ours is the one country that has seen fit to make preserving the memory of the Holocaust a national imperative. When President Jimmy Carter set up the Presidential Commission on the Holocaust in 1978 and appointed me chairman, I was asked about my vision of the future Holocaust Museum. I wrote one sentence, now permanently inscribed on one of its walls: "For the dead and the living, we must bear witness." For not only are we responsible for the memories of the dead, we are also responsible for what we do with those memories.

Words, images, sounds—that is the stuff of memory. Fifty years ago, somewhere in the Carpathian Mountains, a young Jewish woman read in a Hungarian newspaper a brief account of the Warsaw Ghetto uprising. Astonished, dismayed, she wondered aloud: "Why are our Jews in Warsaw behaving like this? Why are they fighting? Couldn't they have waited quietly until the end of the war?"

Treblinka, Ponar, Belzec, Chelmno, Birkenau; she had never heard of those places. One year later, together with her entire family, she was in a cattle car traveling to the Black Hole of History named Auschwitz.

But those places, and others, were known to officials in Washington and London, Moscow and Stockholm, Geneva and the Vatican. After all, by April 1943 nearly 4 million Jews had already perished. The Pentagon knew, the State Department knew, the White House knew, most governments knew; only the victims did not know. Thus the painful question: Why weren't Hungarian Jews, the last remnant of eastern European Jewry, warned of their impending doom?

Jews of every description—old and young, beggars and industrialists, sages and madmen, Ashkenazim from France and Sephardim from Greece, intellectuals from Lithuania and Hasidim from Poland—together began their inexorable journey to a fiery altar of unprecedented dimension. I saw them all, including the children, entering the shadow of flames.

Light is God's shadow, said Giordano Bruno, the Italian philosopher who was burned at the stake in Rome four centuries ago. I say: No. It is fire that is His shadow, the *fire* that consumed a third of a people whose memory of God is the most ancient in recorded history.

Inside the Kingdom of Night, we tried to understand and could not. We found ourselves in an unfamiliar world, a creation parallel to God's, with its own hierarchy, its own princes and hangmen, its own laws and customs. There were only two categories: those who were there to kill and those who were there to be killed.

In Poland, SS officers used Jewish infants for target practice. The only emotion they ever showed was anger when they missed.

In Kiev, an SS officer beheaded two Jewish children in front of their mother. In anguish, she held them close and began to dance.

In Romania, the Iron Guard killed Jews and displayed them in butcher shops with signs: "Kosher Meat."

As you walk through the Holocaust Museum, as you look into the eyes of the killers and their victims, ask yourselves: How could the murderers do what they did and go on living? Why was Berlin encouraged in its belief that it could decree with impunity the humiliation, persecution, extermination of an entire people? Why weren't the railways leading to Birkenau bombed by Allied planes? Why was there no outcry, no public indignation?

Another question: Where did the poorly armed fighters in the ghettos and the forests find the courage to take on the mightiest legions in Europe?

And the most awesome question of all: Why was man's silence matched by God's?

The questions, in fact, are endless and will forever remain unanswered. Indeed, if there is an answer to the Holocaust, it must—by definition—be the wrong answer. Nor is the Museum an answer; it is but a question mark.

Every event connected with that period defies human understanding. It is not because I cannot explain, that you will not understand; it is because you will not understand, that I cannot explain.

The essence of this tragedy is that it can never be fully communicated.

In one of my tales, an SS officer derides a young yeshiva[1] student, telling him that if he happened to survive, his words would fall on deaf ears: "Some will laugh at you," he says. "Others will try to redeem themselves through you . . . People will refuse to believe you. You will possess the truth; but it will be the truth of a madman."

And yet, we are duty-bound to try. Not to do so would mean to forget. To forget would mean to kill the victims a second time. We could not prevent their first death; we must not allow them to vanish again. Memory is not only a victory over time, it is also a triumph over injustice.

That is one of the lessons we have learned. There are others. We have learned that though the Holocaust was principally a Jewish tragedy, its implications are universal. Though not all victims were Jewish, all Jews were victims.[2] We have learned that whatever happens to one community ultimately affects every community. Anti-Semitism is the beginning, not the end, of a disease. Prejudice knows no boundaries. When children are killed in Bosnia, it is our humanity that has failed. When people massacre one another in India, it is our fault too. We have learned that although every human being has the right to be different, none has the right to be indifferent to suffering.

Nevertheless, hatred continues to cause so much suffering in the world today. Religious hatred, ethnic hatred, racial hatred.

Let us therefore seize this moment to condemn the scourge of anti-Semitism, bigotry, and hatred. The bloodshed in Bosnia has to be stopped. We cannot tolerate the excruciating sights of this old new war. I was in the former Yugoslavia last fall. I cannot sleep remembering what I have seen. As a Jew I am saying that we have to do something to stop

1 **yeshiva:** Jewish school.

2 **victims:** Six million Jews died during the Holocaust. Five million "undesirables" also died: Gypsies, Jehovah's Witnesses, communists and political prisoners, homosexuals, and the handicapped.

the killing in that country. People fight each other and children die. Why? Something—anything—must be done to stop the bloodshed there. It will not stop unless we stop it.

Remember the loving yet naïve woman, somewhere in the Carpathians, who together with most Jews of her town perished in a tempest of fury and fire?

She was my mother. ∾

IN THE CONCENTRATION CAMP 1941 George Grosz

Genocide in Bosnia

Nazi Survivors See Specter of Holocaust in Bosnia's Camps

MARY ANN LICKTEIG

Des Moines Register Staff Writer

August 23, 1992—A bony man with a shaved head and sunken eyes stares from the front page of a newspaper, and David Fishel can't look. More eyes flash on the television screen and Morris and Sally Wolf have to change the channel.

"When we watch this," Sally Wolf explains, "I can see my brothers."

Linda Fishman makes herself watch. "I just kind of harden up," she says. "I psych myself up and I say, 'You are not going to cry.' You know? You have to watch it and see what's going on."

A U.S. report estimates that 35,000 people have died in Bosnia, most of them in forced evacuations of Muslim villages.[1]

The Associated Press says two Senate Foreign Relations committee investigators spent a week in the former Yugoslavia and wrote the report. They found evidence of organized killings, rapes, beatings and starvation in detention camps run by Serbs.

They heard about a camp in Brcko, where most of the estimated 1,000 captives were executed over a period of weeks. They listened to a 55-year-old woman describe a make-shift camp in a Trnopolje school, where guards "killed a woman for no reason on the steps of the school. She was going outside to get water for her children."

Footage of such things reminds the Wolfs' son Abe of Holocaust documentaries. "To see it in color, in the news, it's like someone went in and took scenes from World War II and colorized them."

The scenes throw Holocaust survivors into emotional turmoil. They see the world condemning Serbian persecutors, but when it was the Jewish people suffering in World War II, they say, the world did nothing.

"The world let us die," says one.

And while Holocaust survivors empathize with the Bosnian Muslims, they remember that Bosnian Muslims collaborated with the Nazis. They suffered at the hands of Bosnian Muslims.

So some survivors have difficulty feeling for them now, says Fishel, who lives in Windsor Heights [a suburb of Des Moines, Iowa].

---

1 By 1995, when the war for independence for Bosnian Muslims came to an end, more than 100,000 people had died.

Father and son leave a war-torn Croatian village, 1991.

and her parents—died in the war. Now she is 65 and lives in Windsor Heights.

"There is nothing worse than starvation; that's why I say we have to feed these people," she says. But she doesn't think the U.S. military should get involved. "To me, it looks like another Vietnam."

A Windsor Heights man says the world should pull out all stops. "We have to do anything. We send in troops because of oil, and here, people are dying," says the man, who asked not to be named. "I try to live a normal life," he explains.

He spent three years in a Lithuanian ghetto and months at the Dachau concentration camp, but some of his friends and co-workers don't know.

He understands; he was imprisoned in six camps. One of the men dangling outside his window at Blehamer was the father of one of his best friends.

"I understand that they are hurt," he says. "I am hurt, too. But we have to put a stop to hurt, you see? We have to start somewhere."

All survivors interviewed agreed.

"I would like them to have food," says Fishman, who was about 13 when the Germans invaded Szydlowiec, Poland, the town where she lived. Her entire family—four older sisters, two younger brothers

Treatment of Bosnian Muslims is unconscionable, he says. "And because they are European, the world is in an uproar. How about in Africa?"

And what about the My Lai massacre, he asks. "Our boys did the same things—run in villages and kill people. For what?"

Jacob Waizman, a 72-year-old Des Moines man who was imprisoned for all of World War II, says, "Something has to be done to save humanity."

To say these people are scarred for life is an understatement.

Fishel still wakes up sweating and screaming and crying. He is 63 years old now. He has two grown daughters and four grandchildren. But he can still hear his mother screaming as the soldiers ripped him from her arms. It was the last time he saw her.

Physically, too, he is scarred. His prisoner number—184570—was tattooed on his left arm at Blehamer, a subsidiary of Auschwitz. He used to wish he could make it go away. Now, he says, "I just don't pay any attention to it."

Waizman has a bump on his head where he says Josef Mengele, the infamous Nazi doctor, hit him with a rifle because he didn't want to leave his mother. He has a bullet in his left leg and a white scar where another bullet hit his right leg. He was shot on a march from Hirshberg to Buchenwald because he wasn't walking fast enough.

He has nightmares, too.

His mother's last words to him when he was forced from her arms were, "Jacob, my son." When he was liberated 5½ years later, he weighed 60 pounds, was lying on top of dead bodies and was picked out by American soldiers because they saw him move. He had nearly died several times before that.

Three times came during roll call at Hirshberg. When the soldiers ordered, "Hats down," prisoners had to take off their hats in unison. Whoever was too slow or too fast was shot. One Sunday, Waizman thought it was his hat that slapped late. The soldier motioned, and he stepped forward. But the soldier said, "Nein, die andere," which means, "No, the other."

At other roll calls, the soldiers shot every 20th person. One time Waizman was No. 18; another time, he was No. 21.

At another camp, he was ordered to dig his own grave. He did, but before he was shot, his work foreman intervened.

When ordered to the Buchenwald gas chambers in a group of 25, Waizman and a friend lagged behind. When they were out of the perimeter of the observation tower's spotlight, they hit the ground and crawled to safety.

Sally and Morris Wolf of West Des Moines kept their past from their children as long as they could. She lost her entire family. He lost everyone—including his first wife and a child—except for one brother. They didn't tell the children until the children started to ask why they didn't have grandparents.

Even as adults, son Abe says, he and his two brothers have heard little about the war. He finds the scenes from Bosnia eerie. They look like Nazi concentration camps to him, but he does not worry about his parents seeing them.

"Obviously, they are survivors," he says. "They are the strongest people in the world."

More Than an Ounce Required

In 2008, an organization called the Genocide Prevention Project issued a report titled "More than an Ounce Required: Summoning the Political Will to Prevent Genocide and Mass Atrocity Crimes in the 21st Century." The report identifies 1) warning signs of a potential genocide, 2) countries at high risk for genocide in the near future, and 3) recommendations to world leaders on how to prevent the unspeakable tragedies of mass atrocity. The selection that follows is from the introductory summary.

A New Paradigm[1] for Prevention

Is it possible to forecast where, and even when, the tragedies of genocide or ethnic cleansing might occur?

This report indicates that the answer is yes.

Just as a change in the barometric pressure can be one indicator of a coming storm, so can political instability, rising ethnic tensions, incitement to hate, and economic and political discrimination, among other factors, signal the potential for systematic violence against civilians on a mass scale.

The places where systematic slaughter of civilians is happening or could happen are, actually, fairly well known.

But knowledge alone is insufficient to save lives. Little good is achieved, for example, if scientists believe a hurricane is imminent but fail to communicate this fact to officials who can raise the alarm, evacuate those threatened, and coordinate necessary aid.

The recent tragedies of Darfur, Rwanda, Cambodia, and Bosnia and Herzegovina[2] all bear witness to the international community's failure to prevent systematic mass atrocity crimes (defined here as ethnic cleansing, war crimes, crimes against humanity, and genocide). And yet, in the lead-up to each of these crises the warning signs were clear.

Going forward, the international community must heed such early warning signs, and be prepared to act quickly and effectively when the indicators show the potential for systematic atrocities.

---

1 **paradigm:** model or framework.

2 See pages 136–137 for more information on these atrocities.

This requires that international leaders adopt a new framework, one focused on prevention. A prevention framework would have two central components:

- An early warning system to signal an escalation[3] of the most serious human rights abuses against civilians based on characteristics of their identity such as race, ethnicity, tribal affiliation, or religion.

- Well-coordinated and active diplomacy in the earliest stages of a brewing crisis, undertaken with the intention of averting an escalation of violence.

Such diplomatic actions—those well short of any military action—could be undertaken by the UN or individuals or groups of member states and could include both "carrots" and "sticks."

It is the contention of this report that once civilians are being attacked, the international community is obligated to protect them from systematic mass killing.

Working to prevent or avert tragedy is not only humane, it is pragmatic. In addition to the bloody toll in human lives and suffering, atrocity crimes can bring an increase in global insecurity and the potential for regional destabilization. Furthermore, the economic cost of an intervention is more burdensome once violence has escalated.

The task at hand is, admittedly, difficult. Great challenges accompany any effort to change long-standing grievances or to improve international collaboration on issues of peace. But genocide, ethnic cleansing, war crimes, and crimes against humanity are the worst forms of mass barbarity. These are crimes that the international community is morally and legally obligated to address, not as an afterthought but as a priority.

This report calls for a new level of global and national leadership to prevent mass atrocity crimes, one marked by a willingness to act at the earliest stages to avert humanitarian catastrophe—rather than, as we have many times in the past, ignoring the warning signs and then watching as tragedy unfolds. ∾

---

3 **escalation:** increase or heightening.

GENOCIDES IN THE 20TH AND 21ST CENTURIES

In the wake of the genocide, Armenian child refugees crowd the classrooms of Syria.

Armenia (1915–1918)
Ottoman authorities massacre 1.5 million Armenians.

Holocaust (1938–1945)
Nazis kill 6 million Jews.

Cambodia (1975–1979)
Khmer Rouge (Cambodian communists) kill 2 million Cambodians of Chinese descent.

Jews in the Warsaw Ghetto in Poland are deported in crowded freight cars to the gas chambers of Treblinka.

Students view photographs of the victims of the Khmer Rouge brutality at the Tuol Sleng Museum, once the site of a secret prison.

Risk Factors and Other Early Warning Signs

Just as there are risk factors for illness—for instance, obesity is a risk factor for heart disease—there are indicators of the human rights abuses that can lead to systematic mass atrocity crimes. With the caveat that not every risk factor is present in every humanitarian crisis, warning signs for atrocity crimes include:

- Divisions within society by group, which may include exclusionary ideology;

- Economic and political discrimination against specific groups;

- Human flight and movement of refugees or internally displaced persons;

- Prior history of genocide or a legacy of vengeance-seeking for group grievances; and

- Ideological character of the ruling party, including incitement to hate.

Srebrenica (1995)
Bosnian Serb Army massacres 8,000 Muslim men and boys, part of a larger war in Bosnia and Herzegovina that took more than 100,000 lives between 1992 and 1995.

Rwanda (1994)
Governing Hutu massacre about 800,000 civilians, almost all belonging to the minority Tutsi ethnic group.

Darfur (2003–present)
Sudan government assaults rebel groups in the Darfur region of the country. Estimates of deaths range from 50,000 to more than 400,000.

Gravestones mark the tragedy of the Srebrenica massacre.

Trucks bring in much needed supplies to Rwandan refugees who had to flee to Zaire.

Open Letter to World Leaders

Under the Genocide Prevention Project's name, survivors of 20th- and 21st-century genocides also issued an "Open Letter to World Leaders" urging them with the voices of the victims themselves to renew a commitment to preventing genocide.

December 9, 2008

An Open Letter to World Leaders,

We are survivors of the genocides that have forever stained our nations, torn apart our communities and families, and lacerated[4] our souls. We call upon you, our leaders, to direct your highest purpose toward ending forever the agonies of mass atrocity crimes.

We approach you on behalf of our beloved dead; in their millions of voices. Brutality and violence are muting the voices of our sisters and brothers in places like Darfur, Somalia, Burma, and Congo,[5] yet we can hear their pleas for protection, and we must speak for them too. We speak for the world's children and for generations yet to come; for unless we take responsible action now, they too, in countless numbers, will pay the ultimate price.

Sixty years ago, on December 9, 1948, the world, through the United Nations, committed itself to prevent and punish the crime of genocide.

In 2005 this obligation was unanimously reaffirmed by the international community in the World Summit Outcome Document, which states that when nations manifestly[6] fail to protect their populations, we, as an international community, "are prepared to take collective action."

These words and our responsibility could not be clearer, yet over and over again we have witnessed the tragic failures of the international community to protect its most vulnerable populations. We speak from

4 **lacerated:** ripped or torn; caused deep emotional pain.

5 **Somalia, Burma, and Congo:** Somalia and Congo in Africa and Burma (Myanmar) in the Indian subcontinent are places where human rights violations and mass atrocities have been committed.

6 **manifestly:** obviously.

Rwanda, from Cambodia, from Bosnia and Herzegovina, from Armenia, from the Diaspora[7] of the Holocaust, and from the flames of Darfur. We speak because we know that until the world makes this commitment absolute, we are destined to repeat the most shameful chapters in human history.

Darfur

Niemat Ahmadi, at-large member of the Darfuri Leaders' Network

Salih Mahmoud Osman, Sudan Organization Against Torture, Recipient of the Sakharov Prize

Armenia

Adriyan Bagciyan
Arsalos Dadir
Onorik Eminian
Perouz Kalousdian
Charlotte Kechejian
Onorik Eminian
Beba Hadzic
Alice Shnorhokian

Holocaust

Ruth R. Cohen
Marcel Drimer
Ania Drimer
Gina Lanceter
Louise Lawrence-Israels, Holocaust survivor from the Netherlands
Margit Meissner
Jonas Weiss
Susan Weiss

Srebrenica

Hingeni Evernsel, Founder and director of BOSFAM[8]

Hatidza Mehmedovic, President of the "Srebrenica-mothers" in Srebrenica

Rwanda

Benoit Kaboyi, on behalf of the umbrella organization representing survivors of the Rwandan Genocide (Ibuka) Ibuka Executive Secretary

Jacqueline Murekatete, Rwandan survivor and Human Rights Activist, Jacqueline's Human Rights Corner

Cambodia

Socheata Poeuv, child of Cambodian survivors, Executive Director, Khmer Legacies

Theary Seng, Executive Director of the Center for Social Development

Sichan Siv, Former US Ambassador to the UN

---

4 **Diaspora:** places around the world where Jews have dispersed.

5 **BOSFAM:** An organization that provides support and assistance to women affected by the Bosnian War.

Vigil for Darfur

BY Sabina Carlson

Hold up your candle if you are an angel.
Hold up your candle if the light of hope
dances and curls about your spine
like the breath of light
about the wick.

Or blow out your candle if you believe
that when
these flames flicker out
we will forget
the faces we now see before us:
the faces
of the hopeful,
and the memory of the abused.

Hold up your candle
if the people standing alongside you
have become your wings,
so that
side by side
we fly
to a better place and time.

Hold up your candle if you know that sound
does not travel
through air and wires but rather through the
chords
of our hearts and that we will never
be able to claim
that we could not hear
a single cry
because a deafening ocean
stood between us.

Hold up your candle if you remember
how the world forgot 800
thousand Rwandans,
hold up your candle if you have a hole
burnt into your heart

by the Shoah,[1] the Great Fire,
the Holocaust
and hold up your candle if you can still see
the smoke
and taste the ashes.

Hold up your candle
if you know
that tears
only feed
that fire.

And hold up your candle
if you refuse to let the world
sob itself to sleep, waiting for a wish,
because we did not listen to them,
because we did not burn with them,
because we did not tell them
"I am
going
to save you.
Here,
I am your miracle."

For who
dares to say that miracles are simply
the dusted spines
of Bibles?
Friends, look
at the crying wings you stand
side by side with, listen to the heavenly
psalms of hope and hurt, feel your heart
rise
through the halo above your head
to join with a hundred thousand others
who will heal
this world.
hold up your candle
if you
are an angel.

1 **Shoah:** Hebrew word meaning "catastrophe" and used to refer to
the killing of millions of European Jews during World War II;
Holocaust.

RESPONDING TO CLUSTER FIVE

ESSENTIAL QUESTION:
GIVEN THE HISTORY OF PREJUDICE IN THE UNITED STATES, COULD A HOLOCAUST HAPPEN HERE?

The last group of selections in this book provides an opportunity for independent learning and the application of critical thinking skills. There are many options that you can use to show you have mastered these skills. Here are three possibilities. Your teacher may provide others.

1. Break into small groups, with each group taking responsibility for teaching a part of the final cluster. Your lesson might include one of the following:

   a) create discussion questions and lead a discussion

   b) develop vocabulary activities

   c) prepare a test for the cluster selections.

   As you develop your activity, remember the essential question stated above.

2. Write a research paper on a topic related to the Holocaust.

3. Individually or in small groups, develop an independent project that demonstrates your knowledge of or feelings about the Holocaust. For example, you could create a song, music video, dance, poem, performance, drama, or artistic rendering that reflects your feelings about the Holocaust.

CLOSE READING

Re-reading, we find a new book. —Mason Cooley

Close reading is the careful interpretation of a text. Re-reading is the key strategy for close reading. The "new book" readers often encounter on re-reading is layered with meaning.

There is no single right way to do a close reading of a text. The following general process, however, presents three broad stages or levels in re-reading that build on one another to help produce a deep understanding of a text.

1. First Readings: Build Understanding

On a first reading, focus on grasping the literal or explicit meaning of a text. Answer the questions as you read, paraphrase key ideas, and jot down any questions you have.

Informational Text	
Questions to Ask	**Where to Look for Answers**
What is the main idea?	Title, introduction, or first few paragraphs
What information backs up the main idea?	Body paragraphs, especially their topic sentences
How are the ideas in the text related to one another?	Transitions between sections/ideas
What conclusion does the writer draw, and how does it relate to the main idea and supporting ideas?	Concluding paragraphs

Argumentative Text	
Questions to Ask	**Where to Look for Answers**
What is the main claim, or point the writer is trying to prove?	Title, introduction, or first few paragraphs
What evidence does the writer provide to back up that claim?	Body paragraphs, especially their topic sentences
What counterclaims, if any, does the writer address?	Body paragraphs, often marked with such words and phrases as "in contrast," "despite," "while it is true that"
How are the ideas in the text related to one another?	Transitions between sections/ideas
What conclusion does the writer draw, and how does it relate to the main claim and supporting ideas?	Concluding paragraphs

Narrative Text	
Questions to Ask	**Where to Look for Answers**
What event starts the narrative in motion?	Introduction or first few paragraphs
What is the setting of the narrative?	Introduction and throughout
Who are the people or characters in the narrative?	Introduction and throughout
What problem do the people or characters face?	Introduction and throughout
What happens to the people or characters as the narrative unfolds?	Body paragraphs
What is the outcome or resolution of the narrative?	Concluding paragraphs

Poetry	
Questions to Ask	**Where to Look for Answers**
If the poem tells a story, what is the basic outline of that story?	Throughout
What is the tone of the poem?	Throughout
What images, words, or ideas stand out as striking?	Throughout
What images, words, or ideas are repeated, if any?	Throughout
What message do you see in the poem?	Title, throughout

2. Focused Re-readings: Analyze the Text and Gather Evidence

Re-reading after you have grasped a basic understanding of a text is the stage at which you are most likely to encounter that "new book" referred to in the beginning quote, because at this level you analyze the text carefully and focus on details that may bring new meaning to what you have read. The chart below shows some of the points you can focus on in a re-reading of almost any kind of text. It also shows what questions you can ask and where and how you can discover the answers to those questions.

Focused Re-reading		
Focus and Thinking Skills	**Questions to Ask**	**Finding Textual Evidence**
Author's purpose, such as to inform, put forward an argument, entertain, satirize, tell a story *Thinking skills: Recognize explicit statements; draw inferences about implied purpose(s)*	Why did the writer write this? Is the purpose stated explicitly or is it only implied?	Look in the title and beginning paragraphs for quotes that show the answers to your questions.

continued

Focused Re-reading *(cont.)*		
Focus and Thinking Skills	**Questions to Ask**	**Finding Textual Evidence**
Word choice and style, including length of sentences, variety of sentence beginnings, and variety of sentence types *Thinking skills: Analyze; break passages down by word choice and sentence style and look for patterns*	What words and phrases caught your attention for their strength and clarity? Does the author tend to use long sentences, short sentences, or a variety of sentence lengths? Do the sentences begin in a variety of ways (for example, subject first, prepositional phrase first, etc.)?	Look throughout for examples that demonstrate the results of your analysis (for example, three vivid word choices, three varied sentence patterns, etc.). In a long text, examine a section from the beginning, two or three sections from the middle, and a section from the end.
Figurative language, such as similes, metaphors, hyperbole, alliteration *Thinking skills: Analyze to identify figures of speech; classify the type of figurative language; compare figurative language to a possible replacement in literal language*	What figures of speech does the writer use? What do they accomplish that literal language would not?	Look throughout, but especially in descriptive passages, for various examples of figurative language and compare them to literal language.
Structure, including main sections and such organizational patterns as chronological order and order of importance *Thinking skills: Analyze to identify the sections of a text; classify to determine the organizational pattern*	What are the main sections of the text? What is the organizational pattern of the text?	Look throughout the text for transitional words and phrases that show both where sections break and how they are connected. Identify the main ideas from each section.
Point of view in fiction, including choice of narrator *Thinking skills: Analyze narrative to identify point of view; compare points of view by imagining a passage told from a different point of view and evaluating the effect.*	Is the story told from the first- or third-person point of view? If it is not in first-person, how much does the narrator know about the characters? What effect does the choice of narrative point of view have on the text? Why might the author have chosen that point of view?	Look for pronouns. If the narrator refers to himself or herself as "I," the story is in first-person. Look at key passages in which important information is revealed for examples that show the effect of point of view on the narrative.

continued

Focused Re-reading (cont.)		
Focus and Thinking Skills	**Questions to Ask**	**Finding Textual Evidence**
Point of view in nonfiction, including frame of reference, such as scientist, parent, teenager *Thinking skills: Recognize explicit statements; draw inferences about the writer from telling details*	What is the writer's frame of reference?	Look in the introduction and body paragraphs for details that give insight into the writer's experience, worldview, and possible bias.
Implied meanings *Thinking skills: Analyze details; draw inferences and conclusions*	What is left unsaid? What inference can you draw from a collection of details when you "read between the lines"?	Look throughout for details that "show" not "tell." In fiction these would include the actions of the characters and details of the setting. In nonfiction, these might appear in descriptive passages where the reader is left to draw his or her own conclusions. Find examples that support your interpretation of the implied meaning.

Different kinds of texts suggest additional points to focus on during re-reading.

Focused Re-Reading of Informational and Argumentative Text		
Focus and Thinking Skills	**Questions to Ask**	**Finding Textual Evidence**
Clarification and verification of information *Thinking skills: Define key terms; analyze complicated sentences and paragraphs; compare to other sources to verify information*	What parts confused you? What did you not understand well on first reading? What seemed to contradict information you thought you knew?	Look in passages that raised questions in your mind in first reading; refer to outside sources if necessary for confirming or contradicting information.
Assumptions *Thinking skills: Logical thinking to evaluate the assumption underlying the claim*	Does every claim depend on a valid assumption?	Look for passages that put forward claims in an argument; look for examples, if any, of hidden assumptions.

continued

Focused Re-Reading of Informational and Argumentative Text (cont.)		
Focus and Thinking Skills	**Questions to Ask**	**Finding Textual Evidence**
Development of an argument and key supporting ideas *Thinking skills: Evaluate the relevance, sufficiency, and importance of the supporting details; distinguish fact from opinion*	By what method does the writer attempt to prove his or her point? Are the supporting ideas relevant and sufficient to prove the point?	Look throughout for all the facts, reasons, and examples offered in support of each claim and/or counterclaim.
Style and tone *Thinking skills: Analyze language choices; evaluate appropriateness*	Is the style formal and respectful, or informal and full of "loaded" language (words that carry strong, usually negative connotations)?	Look throughout, but especially at the beginning and ending where the author wants to make his or her point most strongly, for examples that show formal, respectful language or disrespectful loaded language.

Focused Re-reading of Fiction and Drama		
Focus and Thinking Skills	**Questions to Ask**	**Finding Textual Evidence**
Plot *Thinking skills: Sequence; draw inferences; examine cause-effect relationships*	What is the impact of each main development of the plot on the characters?	Look for examples of characters' words or actions before a turning point in the story and after a turning point.
Setting *Thinking skills: Draw inferences*	How does the setting contribute to the mood of the story? How do the details of the setting help define characters?	Look for descriptive details throughout the story about the time and physical characteristics of the place of the events and their impact on mood and characters.
Characters *Thinking skills: Analyze details of characterization; generalize from details; draw inferences from details*	How does each character contribute to the development of the plot? How do the details of characterization and the dialogue reveal the characters' personalities and motivations? Why do characters act as they do?	Look throughout for character 1) descriptions, 2) thoughts, 3) words, 4) actions, 5) changes, 6) motivations.
Theme *Thinking skills: Draw inferences; generalize from details; synthesize various elements*	How does the author communicate the theme through the development of setting, characters, and plot? What passages and details in the story best express the main theme?	Look for passages and details from each main part of the story or drama that express theme.

Focused Re-reading of Poetry		
Focus and Thinking Skills	**Questions to Ask**	**Finding Textual Evidence**
Persona (the poet's "voice") *Thinking skills: Analyze; draw inferences*	How does the persona relate to the subject, mood, and theme of the poem?	Look for specific examples that show the persona's involvement and reveal attitudes.
Meter and rhyme *Thinking skills: Analyze meter and rhyme; synthesize to assess their effect*	How do the meter and rhyme affect the rhythm and mood of the poem?	Look for metrical patterns and rhyme schemes from several places in the poem.
Sound devices, such as alliteration, assonance, onomatopoeia *Thinking skills: Analyze language; classify types of sound devices; draw inferences about their meaning and effect*	What sound devices are in the poem? What effect do they have?	Look throughout the poem for examples of sound devices in relation to other elements of the poem.
Theme *Thinking skills: Draw inferences; generalize from details; synthesize various elements*	How does the poet communicate the theme through the details of the poem?	Look for passages and details from throughout the poem that express theme.

3. Synthesis: Evaluate the Text

By now you may have encountered the "new book" that close reading often reveals, a text with layers of meaning. On later re-readings, you can stand back from the text and begin to see it from a critic's point of view. Following are some of the criteria by which any great work of literature, or classic, is usually judged. When you evaluate a literary work, nonfiction or fiction, consider the following characteristics.

Some Characteristics of Great Literature

- Explores great themes in human nature and the human experience that many people can identify with—such as growing up, family life, personal struggles, or war
- Expresses universal values—such as truth or hope—to which people from many different backgrounds and cultures can relate
- Conveys a timeless message that remains true for many generations of readers
- Presents vivid impressions of characters, settings, and situations that many generations of readers can treasure
- Demonstrates outstanding and inventive understanding of important aspects of humanity and society

The chart below shows some questions you can ask—and answer with evidence from the text—when you are evaluating a text.

Questions for Evaluating a Text	
Informational Text	How effectively has the writer • presented a clear explanation on a topic of value • used examples and other supporting details • accurately conveyed information • structured the explanation • used language and style to add clarity and life • presented an unbiased view • engaged the reader
Argumentative Writing	How effectively has the writer • presented a clear position or claim on a subject of importance • used examples and other details to support claims • accurately conveyed information • addressed counterclaims • used logic • covered the topic in sufficient depth and breadth • been fair-minded • structured the argument • used language and style to add clarity and life • convinced you
Fiction and Drama	How effectively has the writer • drawn well-rounded characters worth getting to know • developed and paced a plot • set mood and tone • used language • structured the story • developed a meaningful theme
Poetry	How effectively has the poet • used (or not used) rhyme • created stunning word pictures • used figurative language • structured the poem • expressed an otherwise inexpressible idea

USING TEXTUAL EVIDENCE

Prove it! Anytime you write a literary analysis, informational text, or argument, you will be expected to prove your main idea or claim. You draw the **textual evidence** for that proof from the collection of details you have mined during your close readings.

During your close readings, you gathered evidence by taking notes from the work itself. These notes may have included descriptive passages, lines of dialogue, narrative details, facts, examples, statistics, and other kinds of details. In drafting an analysis of a text or in piecing together an informational or argumentative text from several sources, include the evidence in a way that will convince readers of your main idea or claim.

Strengthen your arguments by using relevant quotations from your text or texts that support a point. Work them smoothly into your writing and punctuate them correctly. The following guidelines show how to work textual evidence into a written analysis. They use examples from a literary analysis on a short story by Marjorie Kinnan Rawlings called "A Mother in Mannville."

Guidelines for Using Direct Quotations in a Literary Analysis

1. Always enclose direct quotations in quotation marks.
2. Follow the examples below when writing quotations in different positions in the sentence. Notice that quotations in the middle or end of a sentence are not ordinarily capitalized.

   Begins Sentence   "He wore overalls and a torn shirt," observes the narrator (323).

   Interrupts Sentence   In his "grave gray-blue eyes," the narrator sees a rare and precious quality (325).

   Ends Sentence   The narrator feels that Jerry's integrity makes him "more than brave (325)."

3. Use ellipses—a series of three dots (. . .)—to show that words have been left out of a quotation.

   "For a moment, finding that he had a mother shocked me . . . and I did not know why it disturbed me" (327).

4. If the quotation is four lines or longer, set it off by itself without quotation marks. Indent one inch on the left and leave space above and below it.

   > And after my first fury at her—we did not speak of
   > her again—his having a mother, any sort at all, not far
   > away, in Mannville, relieved me of the ache I had had
   > about him. . . . He was not lonely. It was none of my
   > concern. (328)

5. After each quotation cite the page number of the text in parentheses. The citation usually precedes punctuation marks such as periods, commas, colons, and semicolons. For plays or long poems, also give main divisions, such as the act and scene of the play or the part of the poem, plus line numbers.

Following are examples of using textual evidence in a different kind of writing—an informational research report on the lost city of Atlantis. The sources are indicated in parentheses and would be keyed to a works-cited page at the end of the report.

Examples of Using Textual Evidence in an Informational Report

1. Use a quotation to finish a sentence you have started.

    Example   Photographs taken in 1977 of underwater stones are believed to "bear the mark of human handiwork" (Whitney).

2. Quote a whole sentence. If you omit words from a sentence, indicate the omission with an ellipsis, a series of three dots (. . .).

    Example   "He suggests that the structures match the description in Plato's Dialogue Critias . . . and that the high mountains of Atlantis are actually those of the Sierra Morena and the Sierra Nevada" (Shermer).

3. Quote four or more lines from a source. For a quotation of this length, skip two lines and set the quotation as a block indented one inch on the left. You do not need quotation marks for such an extended quotation.

    Example   Here is how Plato describes the downfall of Atlantis in the dialogue called *Timaeus:*
    Some time later excessively violent earthquakes and floods occurred, and after the onset of an unbearable day and a night, your entire warrior force sank below the earth all at once, and the Isle of Atlantis likewise sank below the sea and disappeared. (1232)

4. Quote just a few words.

    Example   According to Plato, in an "unbearable day and a night" Atlantis was destroyed (*Timaeus* 1232).

5. Paraphrase information from a source.

    Example   "Although many have dismissed Atlantis as a myth, some 50,000 volumes have been written to describe and locate it." [Original]
    Curiosity about Atlantis and efforts to locate it gave rise to some 50,000 books on the topic ("Greek Backs Plato Theory"). [paraphrase]

For informational and argumentative texts, including research reports, be sure to verify factual evidence in your sources for accuracy.

Verifying Factual Evidence

- Locate at least two sources that contain the same basic facts.
- Skim each source for specific details, such as dates, locations, and statistics.
- If the specific details in both sources agree, you can probably rely on their accuracy.
- Watch for discrepancies in broader concepts, such as in the sequence of events or in the relationship between cause and effect.
- If you discover discrepancies, use a third source to determine which source is likely to be more accurate.

COMPARING TEXTS

Another way to achieve a deep understanding of a text is to compare it to another text. You can compare and contrast literary texts in many ways. You could, for example, do a close reading of two (or more) texts using any of the same focus points outlined on pages 144–148, and then compare and contrast the way each text addresses that focus point. Following are just a few of many examples.

Two or More Texts of This Type	Focus Points to Compare and Contrast
Short stories	Structure (use of chronological order or flashbacks), theme, plot, character development, point of view, setting, style
Poems	Role of persona, figurative language, rhyme and meter, theme
Biographies	Details of life that are emphasized or omitted in each version; overall sense of person's character and motivation
Informational Texts	Structure, point of view, importance of main idea, support for main idea, language and style, author's purpose, accuracy of information, possible bias
Argumentative Texts	Structure, point of view, significance of main claim, quality of supporting details for claims, logical reasoning, accuracy of information, possible bias, language and style, conclusions

The following chart shows additional ways to compare and contrast texts to deepen your understanding of them.

Types of Texts to Compare	Questions for Comparing Texts
Texts in different forms or genres (such as stories and poems, historical novels and fantasy stories, short stories and novels)	• How is the approach to theme and topic similar in both forms? • How is the approach to theme and topic different in the two forms or genres? • How does their form or genre make these texts unique?
Fictional portrayal of a time, place, or character and a historical account of the same period	• How do authors of fiction use or alter history?
Modern work of fiction versus traditional sources	• In what ways does the modern work draw on themes, patterns of events, or character types from myths, traditional stories, or religious works? • How is the modern work turned into something new and fresh?

continued

Types of Texts to Compare (cont.)	Questions for Comparing Texts (cont.)
Texts from the same era that approach themes differently	• What was the purpose of each text? • What was the writer's frame of reference or worldview? • Whom was the writer addressing ?
Texts from different eras	• What does each text reveal about social attitudes during the time in which it was written?
Different texts by the same author	• What themes appear repeatedly in works by this author? • What changes in style and/or theme, if any, are apparent in later works by the author compared to earlier works?

Comparing Texts in Different Mediums "Texts" do not necessarily need to be written pieces. In fact, comparing texts in different mediums—such as print, audio, and video—can lead to valuable insights.

The following chart shows some questions to ask when comparing and contrasting texts in different mediums.

Reading a Story, Drama, or Poem	Listening to or Viewing an Audio, Video, or Live Version of the Text
• When you read the text, what do you see in your mind's eye? How do you picture the visual images, the characters, and the setting? • What do you hear—what do the characters' voices sound like? • What are the sounds in the setting? • What can you experience reading a text that you cannot experience when viewing or listening to an audio, video, or live version of the text?	• When you listen to an audio version of the text, what do you experience in comparison to when you read it? Are any elements more vivid? less vivid? • When you view a video version of the text, what do you experience in comparison to when you read it? • What can a video provide that a written text cannot? • How does the experience of a live performance differ from reading a text? • What can a live performance offer that reading a text cannot? • How faithful to the original text is the audio, video, or live version? If it differs in significant ways, why do you think the directors and actors made the choices they did to change it?

You know the techniques writers use to make an impression and impact. They include provocative language, narration that can get inside of characters' heads, and plenty of room for the readers' imaginations to fill in visual and auditory details. Understanding the "tools of the trade" of different mediums can help you make clear comparisons and contrasts.

Techniques of Audio	Techniques of Video	Techniques of Stage
• Actual voices and other sounds in the setting • Possibility of music to help create mood • Room for imagination to fill in visual aspects	• Representation of all sounds and visuals; little left to the imagination • Lighting, sound recording, camera angles, color, focus, and special effects all shape the visual message • Use of background music to help create mood • Editing techniques that place one scene next to another to make a comment	• Representation of some sounds and visuals within the limited scope of the stage • Stage directions that tell characters how to interact in each scene • Lighting and other special effects • Live actors creating a sense of immediacy • Use of music

Sometimes you may be asked to **compare a single scene in two different mediums.** For example, a chilling scene in the book *To Kill a Mockingbird* centers on the shooting of a mad dog by mild-mannered lawyer Atticus Finch. If you read that scene carefully in the book and then compared and contrasted it to the same scene in the movie version of the book, you could evaluate what is emphasized or absent in each treatment of the scene.

Sometimes you may be asked to **compare multiple versions of a story, drama, or poem in different mediums.** How does the stage version of *To Kill a Mockingbird* differ from both the print and movie versions? How do the film and stage versions offer different interpretations of the original text?

AUTHOR BIOGRAPHIES

REUBEN AINSZTEIN Born in the 1920s in Wilno, Poland (now Vilnius, Lithuania), Reuben Ainsztein lived through pogroms throughout the 1930s. Denied entry into Polish universities because he was a Jew, he left Poland at age nineteen to study medicine in Belgium. He supported himself by working as a language tutor. After Germany invaded Belgium, he moved on to France, then Spain, where he was captured and sent to a concentration camp. In 1943, he reached England. Knowing that family members had perished in concentration camps, he joined Britain's Royal Air Force, which he felt allowed him "to falsely claim the credit for having risked my life at a time when my own family had known every possible terror and death itself." After serving in the RAF, Ainsztein worked as a journalist specializing in Eastern European affairs. He also wrote books on Polish and Soviet resistance movements and on Polish Jews during World War II. Ainsztein died in 1981.

ELEANOR AYER is a biographer whose subjects have included Charles Dickens, Adolf Hitler, and ordinary people with extraordinary lives. Her book *Parallel Journeys* tells the story of a peace initiative fostered by Helen, a Jewish German girl who survived Auschwitz; and Alfons, a German boy who served in the Hitler Youth.

SABINA CARLSON wrote "Vigil for Darfur" when she was a senior in high school in Plainsboro, New Jersey. A graduate of Tufts University in Massachusetts, she has worked to alleviate problems for people living in areas of crisis, including Darfur and Haiti. She also interned for Physicians for Human Rights, believing strongly in the vital connection between health and human rights.

FIRST LIEUTENANT WILLIAM J. COWLING While William J. Cowling claims to be the first American soldier to enter the Dachau death camp in the last days of World War II, at least one other soldier makes the same claim. The liberators of Dachau—Cowling included—never forgot the horror of what they found.

IDA FINK Born in 1921 in what is now the Ukraine, Ida Fink spent 1941 and 1942 in the Warsaw Ghetto and then escaped. She has lived in Israel since 1957 and now writes autobiographical short stories about the Holocaust she survived. In 1985, Fink won the Anne Frank Prize in literature. Fink's stories divide the world into before and after the Holocaust, but her stories are not merely chronicles of her trauma. Critics find them rich in sensory detail and celebratory toward the eyewitnesses, whom Fink sees as heroes of the Holocaust era.

HAROLD FLENDER His 1963 biography, *Rescue in Denmark*, helped Harold Flender bring international attention to Denmark's historical resistance to anti-Semitism and Nazi rule during the time of the Holocaust. Flender's use of transcribed sources made his book credible as well as captivating in its account of Danish heroism.

EPHIM FOGEL Born in the Ukraine, Ephim Fogel grew up in New York. He served in the United States Army during the 1940s before going back to school to become a professor of English literature. A poet, translator, and literary scholar, Ephim became the chair of the

English Department at Cornell University. He brought to his position a scholar's wisdom, a strong devotion to university life, and a poet's patience and insight. Fogel is best known for his scholarly works, but his poem "Shipment to Maidanek" has been anthologized often. It was one of the first published pieces of literature to deal with the Holocaust.

ARNOLD GEIER was an American soldier stationed in Vienna after World War II. While in Vienna, he broke military rules to help innumerable Holocaust survivors locate and send messages to loved ones around the world.

The **GENOCIDE PREVENTION PROJECT** has worked with genocide survivors and international survivor organizations to generate a public call to world leaders to recognize warning signs and take action. It is an initiative of Public Interest Projects, a public charity in New York.

BERNARD GOTFRYD During World War II, Bernard Gotfryd had a relatively safe job at a photo studio, and his life could have remained quiet. But he risked his life to pass along photos of Nazi atrocities to the Polish resistance. In 1943, he attempted to escape Poland with the help of the resistance, but he was caught and shipped to an extermination camp in Majdanek. From there, he was shipped to five other camps before he was liberated in 1945. Gotfryd moved to the United States in 1947 and found work as a photographer. Two years later, he was drafted into the U.S. Army as a combat photographer. In 1957, Gotfryd accepted a position as a photojournalist for *Newsweek*. He worked there for more than 30 years. Though best known for his photographs, Gotfryd also is respected for his deeply moving fiction.

KITTY HART When she was twelve years old, Kitty Hart's idyllic childhood in a mountain village was transformed by the Nazi invasion of Poland. A captive resident of the Lublin Ghetto, she endured sickness and almost daily raids and also was called upon to smuggle goods in and out of the ghetto, since children were less likely than adults to be noticed. After escaping the ghetto and attempting to escape Poland, Kitty Hart's family was captured and sent to prisons in Halle, Leipzig, Dresden, and then Auschwitz. Kitty and her mother narrowly survived Auschwitz. Eventually, they were able to join relatives in England, who warned them never to speak about what they had been through. Hart waited 40 years to finally tell her story, which helped others understand the importance of telling the truth about the Holocaust.

JACOB G. HORNBERGER Born and raised in Laredo, Texas, Jacob G. Hornberger worked for many years as a trial lawyer. He also has been an adjunct professor of law and economics at the University of Dallas and became an ardent promoter of free markets. In 1989, Hornberger became the founder and president of The Future of Freedom Foundation, which declares a mission "to present an uncompromising moral, philosophical, and economic case for individual freedom, private property, and limited government." Hornberger has been an editor and contributor to several of the foundation's publications. His editorials have appeared in the *Washington Post*, *Charlotte Observer*, and *El Nuevo Miami Herald*, among other publications.

YALA KORWIN Born and raised in Poland, where she developed a love of words and images, Yala Korwin was sent to a labor camp during World War II. After the war, she became a refugee, living in France. In 1956, Korwin and her husband immigrated to the United States, where she enrolled in college as a French major. In her senior year, Korwin discovered in herself a love of poetry. She began to write, first in free verse and then in sonnet form, which she loves for its economy. Many of Korwin's poems illuminate her experience and understanding of the Holocaust, and several have been anthologized. Korwin has been described as being both "passionate and wise about her truth." You can visit Yala Korwin's Web site at www.yalakorwin.com.

BEREK LATARUS Born and raised in Lodz, Poland, Berek Latarus worked with his father in the lumber business there. After Hitler invaded Poland, the Latarus family was confined to the Lodz Ghetto. Latarus was eventually deported to Auschwitz. He managed to survive his internment, but the rest of his family perished in the Holocaust.

LYN LIFSHIN has written more than 100 books of poetry and has given more than 700 readings throughout the United States. She has taught poetry and prose writing at universities, colleges, and high schools, and has won numerous awards for her work. She is so dedicated to the small presses that first published her and that continue to take chances on good poetry that she has been called the "Queen of the Small Presses." Her work is both simple and meaningful, leading some poets and critics to characterize her as "a modern Emily Dickinson."

GAIL NEWMAN not only writes poetry, but she has also conducted poetry workshops for children in the San Francisco Bay area for more than 20 years. She has appeared with some of her students on a televised program about the arts in California. Newman lives with her husband and son in Bernal Heights, California. Her poems cover topics ranging from her family dog to World War II and the Holocaust.

MARTIN NIEMÖLLER The son of a Lutheran pastor, Martin Niemöller was a German naval lieutenant and U-boat commander during World War I. He was ordained as a Lutheran pastor himself in 1924. For a short time, Niemöller was a supporter of Hitler, but he quickly became disillusioned. In fact, he was one of the first Protestant critics of Nazism. He and a few other Lutheran pastors formed a resistance movement within Germany. Niemöller worked tirelessly to resist the Nazis until he was arrested and imprisoned in Sachsenhausen and Dachau concentration camps, yet he always felt he should have done more to oppose Hitler. After the war, he actively promoted the "Stuttgarter Confession of Guilt" and became an outspoken pacifist in favor of reconciliation and disarmament.

JOHN C. PINE has published work touching on topics from American baseball to the Holocaust.

HANS PETER RICHTER Born in Cologne, Germany, and educated in German schools, Hans Peter Richter was a member of Hitler Youth groups. He spent three years in the German army, rising to the rank of lieutenant and receiving several decorations, including the Iron

Cross. He finally came to realize that he had been brainwashed into believing in a sham philosophy. Later, he fictionalized his experience, declaring "I was there. . . . I believed—and I will never believe again." Richter's novel *Friedrich* won the Mildred L. Batchelder Award in 1972 for the most outstanding book originally published in a foreign language. Richter currently lives in Mainz, Germany.

JOHN ROTH is an American author, editor, and professor known internationally for his research and writings on the Holocaust. He has written hundreds of articles and written, co-written, or edited more than 40 books related to the Holocaust and genocide, beginning in 1979 with *Consuming Fire: Encounters with Elie Weisel and the Holocaust.* The selection "Fritz Gerlich's Spectacles" is from a longer work entitled *The Holocaust Chronicle,* a not-for-profit collaborative project whose purpose is to present the best information possible on the Holocaust and share it with the largest possible audience. The entire work and additional resources are online as well, freely available, at http://www.holocaustchronicle.org/.

FRIEDA SINGER is a poet and editor of poetry anthologies. She edited the book *Daughters in High School: An Anthology of Their Work.* Singer won first prize for her free-verse poem "Dimensions of an Island" in the Florida State Writing Competition in 1999. She lives in Flushing, New York.

ISAAC BASHEVIS SINGER Even before he knew how to write, Isaac Bashevis Singer liked holding a pen. Born in Poland, Singer began his writing career as a journalist in Warsaw in the years between the wars. He was influenced by his father, who was a Hassidic rabbi, and his elder brother, who was both a published author and a spiritual mentor to his younger brother. Singer's novel, *Satan in Goray*, written originally in Yiddish, like most of his books, appeared in 1935 when the Nazis were beginning to eye Poland and just before the author immigrated to the United States. Singer became an American citizen in 1943. In 1957, he published *Gimpel the Fool*, his first collection of stories in English. Singer's chief subject was usually the traditional Polish life in various periods of history, largely before the Holocaust. Singer won the Nobel Prize for literature in 1978, but he spoke humbly of his work, maintaining that "a good writer is basically a storyteller, not a scholar or a redeemer of mankind." Singer died in 1991.

ELIE WIESEL Born in Sighet, Transylvania, Elie Wiesel grew up in a small village in Romania. When he was fifteen, he and his family were deported to death camps, where his mother, father, and youngest of three sisters died. After the war, Wiesel studied in Paris, where he became a journalist and, later, a professor. He then moved to the United States, becoming a citizen in 1963. Weisel has written more than 40 books of fiction and nonfiction, and his memoir *Night* has been translated into more than 30 languages. He is the founding president of the Paris-based Universal Academy of Cultures and the chairman of the Elie Wiesel Foundation for Humanity. In 1978, President Jimmy Carter appointed Wiesel chairman of the United States Holocaust Memorial Council. In 1985, he was awarded the Congressional Medal of Freedom and, in 1986, the Nobel Prize for Peace. He is the Andrew Mellon Professor of Humanities at Boston University and lives in New York City with his wife and son.

Acknowledgments

Text Credits CONTINUED FROM PAGE 2   "Broken Glass, Broken Lives" by Arnold Geier. From *Heroes of the Holocaust*, edited by Arnold Geier. Copyright © 1993 by Arnold Geier. Reprinted by permission of Berkley Books, a division of Penguin Putnam.

"Crystal Night" by Lyn Lifshin. Reprinted from *Ghosts of the Holocaust: An Anthology of Poetry by the Second Generation,* edited by Stewart J. Florsheim, by permission of the Wayne State University Press.

"Family Album" by Amos Neufeld. Reprinted from *Ghosts of the Holocaust: An Anthology of Poetry by the Second Generation,* edited by Stewart J. Florsheim, by permission of the Wayne State University Press. First appeared in *Jewish Frontier* (March–April, 1987).

"For the Dead and the Living" by Elie Wiesel. New Leader Adaptation of Mr. Wiesel's address at The U. S. Holocaust Museum's Dedication Ceremony. Reprinted by permission of Georges Borchardt, Inc. for the author.

"Fritz Gerlich's Spectacles" by John Roth. Reprinted from *The Holocaust Chronicle* by permission of Louis Weber, Publications International. Copyright © 2002 by Publications International.

"The Little Boy with His Hands Up" by Yala Korwin. From *Blood to Remember: American Poets on the Holocaust,* edited by Charles Fishman. Copyright © 1982 by Yala Korwin. First appeared in *Martyrdom and Resistance.* Reprinted by permission of the author and the United States Holocaust Memorial Museum.

"Genocide in Bosnia: Nazi survivors see specter of Holocaust in Bosnia's camps" by Mary Ann Lickteig. From the August 23, 1992 issue of *The Des Moines Register.* Copyright © 1992, reprinted with permission by *The Des Moines Register.*

"The Power of Light" from *Stories for Children* by Isaac Bashevis Singer. Copyright © 1984 by Isaac Bashevis Singer. Reprinted by permission of Farrar, Straus & Giroux, Inc.

From *Rescue in Denmark* by Harold Flender. (New York: Simon & Schuster, 1963) Copyright © 1963 by Harold Flender. Reprinted by permission of Georges Borchardt, Inc. for the author.

"Return to Auschwitz" from *Return to Auschwitz* by Kitty Hart. Reprinted by permission of Harold Ober Associates Incorporated. Copyright © 1981 by Kitty Hart.

"Reunions" from *Anton the Dove Fancier* by Bernard Gotfryd. Copyright © 1990 by Bernard Gotfryd. Reprinted by permission of the author.

"Saving the Children" by Frieda Singer. From *Blood to Remember: American Poets on the Holocaust* edited by Charles Fishman. Copyright © 1985 by Frieda Singer. Reprinted by permission of the author.

"Serving Mein Fuhrer" by Eleanor H. Ayer. Reprinted with the permission of Atheneum Books for Young Readers, an imprint of Simon & Schuster Children's Publishing Division, from *Parallel Journeys* by Eleanor H. Ayer with Helen Waterford and Alfons Heck. Copyright © 1995 Eleanor H. Ayer.

"Shipment to Maidanek" by Ephim Fogel. First printed in *Cross Section 1945,* edited by Edwin Seaver, by L. B. Fischer Co. Copyright © 1945, 1957, 1984 by Ephim Fogel. Reprinted by permission of Charlotte Fogel.

"A Spring Morning" from *A Scrap of Time and Other Stories* by Ida Fink. Reprinted by arrangement with Liepman AG, care of Joan Daves Agency as agent for the proprietor. Copyright © 1983 by Ida Fink.

"A Survivor Remembers," the oral history of Berek Latarus. Reprinted with the permission of Macmillan Library Reference U.S.A., a division of Ahsuog, Inc. From *Witnesses to the Holocaust: An Oral History,* edited by Rhoda G. Lewin. Copyright © 1990 by the Jewish Community Relations Council/Anti-Defamation League of Minnesota and the Dakotas.

"The Survivor" by John C. Pine. From *Cliff Walk* (Moveable Feast Press, 1985). Copyright © 1985 by John C. Pine. Reprinted by permission of the author.

From *The Warsaw Ghetto Revolt* by Reuben Ainsztein. Copyright © 1979 by Reuben Ainsztein. Reprinted by permission of Schocken Books, a division of Random House, Inc.

"Vigil for Darfur" by Sabina Carlson. Reprinted by permission of Sabina Carlson.

"The White Rose: A Lesson in Dissent" by Jacob G. Hornberger. Originally appeared in the January 1996 edition of The Future of Freedom Foundation's *Freedom Daily.* Reprinted by permission of the author.

Every reasonable effort has been made to properly acknowledge ownership of all material used. Any omissions or mistakes are not intentional and, if brought to the publisher's attention, will be corrected in future editions.